delicious.

quick smart cook

delicious food without the fuss

delicious.

quick smart cook

delicious food without the fuss

VALLI LITTLE

Photography by Brett Stevens

HarperCollins*Publishers*Ltd

contents

introduction

It's funny how life has dictated that I become a quick smart cook. Quick, because with a busy family life and career, getting a delicious dinner on the table in a hurry every night became a priority. And smart, because over the years I've learned the importance of being a savvy shopper. By buying wisely at the supermarket and adding some lovely fresh ingredients, I've found it's possible to cook uncomplicated, yet creative meals in no time at all.

For most of us, the big question at the end of each day is what to have for dinner, and it's not always easy to come up with something new and interesting.

I have my tried-and-tested favourites that have served me well over the years, but I also enjoy adding a twist to everyday recipes to offer an element of excitement and surprise for family and friends.

Entertaining is much the same – I try to keep the fuss to a minimum, and instead come up with relatively simple ideas that have a wow factor (the peanut butter ice cream with caramel popcorn, for example).

In this book, it's a pleasure to share more than 120 brand-new recipes with you. My inspiration has come from my travels and from the chefs and cooks who I work alongside for *delicious*. magazine, but most of all from the wonderful array of fresh produce that's available to us here in Australia.

Whether you're a seasoned cook in search of inspiration, or a novice looking for easy techniques and time-saving recipes, I hope you'll find it here in *Quick Smart Cook*. So pop on that apron, grab a pan and let's get cooking!

Valli

Crunchy granola

Serves 4

Make a big batch of this moreish toasted muesli so breakfast is at
the ready – it will keep in an airtight container for up to two weeks.

2 cups (180g) rolled oats
2 tbs sesame seeds
¹/₄ cup (40g) sunflower seeds
¹/₄ cup (40g) almonds
¹/₂ cup (50g) walnuts, chopped
3 tbs maple syrup
3 tbs honey
¹/₃ cup (30g) chopped dried apricots
¹/₃ cup (55g) sultanas
Milk, natural yoghurt and fresh fruit,
  to serve

Preheat the oven to 180°C. Line a baking
tray with baking paper.

Place the rolled oats, seeds and nuts
in a bowl and mix well to combine.

Place the maple syrup and honey in a
saucepan and stir over low heat for 1 minute
or until runny and combined (or heat in the
microwave for 1 minute until runny). Pour over
the oat mixture and toss gently to combine.

Tip the mixture onto the tray and bake,
stirring occasionally, for 25-30 minutes
until golden all over. Set aside to cool, then
fold through the apricot and sultanas. Store
in an airtight container until needed.

Serve with milk, yoghurt and fresh fruit.

Caramelised mushrooms with ricotta toasts

Serves 4

Keep things interesting by choosing a range of different mushrooms for this dish.

250g small Swiss brown mushrooms
30g unsalted butter
1 tbs olive oil
4 flat mushrooms, stalks trimmed
¼ firmly packed cup (50g) brown sugar
2 tbs balsamic vinegar
1 tbs chopped oregano leaves,
    plus extra leaves to garnish
4 slices sourdough bread,
    chargrilled or toasted
200g fresh ricotta
1 tbs chopped flat-leaf parsley

Slice half the Swiss brown mushrooms.

Melt the butter with the oil in a frypan over medium heat. Add the flat mushrooms, cap-side down, and cook for 2 minutes or until starting to soften, then add all the Swiss browns. Season well with salt and pepper, then cook for 2-3 minutes until the mushrooms have softened. Transfer the mushrooms to a bowl and set aside.

Add the brown sugar, vinegar and oregano to the frypan and return to medium heat, stirring to dissolve the sugar. Return the mushrooms to the frypan and cook, turning to coat in the sauce, for 1-2 minutes until sticky and caramelised. Stir in the parsley, then serve mushrooms with toast and ricotta, garnished with extra oregano leaves.

Coconut pancakes with banana and creme fraiche

Serves 3-4

3 ripe bananas
4 eggs, separated
1 cup (250ml) coconut milk
1 cup (150g) plain flour, sifted
1 tsp baking powder, sifted
Melted unsalted butter, to grease
Creme fraiche, caramel sauce
   (see Basics, p 246), icing sugar
   and shredded coconut, to serve

Mash 1 banana in a bowl, then set aside.

Place the egg yolks, coconut milk and a pinch of salt in a bowl and whisk until combined. Gently fold in the sifted flour, baking powder and mashed banana until combined.

Whisk the eggwhites in a separate bowl until stiff peaks form, then fold into the batter.

Heat a non-stick frypan over medium-low heat and brush with melted butter. Using a heaped tablespoon of batter for each pancake, add 3-4 spoonfuls to the pan and cook for 2-3 minutes each side until golden and cooked through. Keep the pancakes warm while you continue with the remaining batter to make a total of 9 pancakes.

Slice the remaining bananas. Arrange the pancakes in stacks on serving plates, alternating each layer with banana slices and creme fraiche. Drizzle with caramel sauce, then dust with icing sugar and sprinkle with shredded coconut.

Scandi plate

Serves 6

Scandinavians really know how to do breakfast – with lovely breads, smoked fish, and cheeses that make a refreshing change to our regular weekend fare.

6 slices rye or multigrain bread, toasted
300g beetroot dip
200g hot-smoked trout* or salmon,
   broken into pieces
1/2 cup creme fraiche or sour cream
3 tbs (50g) salmon roe* (optional)
1 punnet mustard cress*

Spread the warm toast with beetroot dip and place on serving plates. Break the fish into bite-sized pieces, discarding skin and bones, and place over the beetroot. Add a dollop of creme fraiche or sour cream, then top with salmon roe. Season with salt and pepper, scatter with the mustard cress and serve.
* Hot-smoked trout is available from delis and supermarkets. Salmon roe is available from delis, gourmet food shops and fishmongers. Mustard cress is available from selected greengrocers and supermarkets.

Berry yoghurt muffins

Makes 6 large muffins

1¹/₂ cups (225g) self-raising flour
¹/₃ cup (30g) rolled oats
3 eggs
³/₄ cup (200g) mixed berry yoghurt
¹/₃ cup (80ml) sunflower oil
1 firmly packed cup (200g) brown sugar
300g frozen raspberries
Icing sugar, to dust

Preheat the oven to 200°C. Grease a 6-hole, ³/₄ cup (185ml) capacity Texas muffin pan.

Place the flour, oats and a pinch of salt in a bowl and mix well.

Beat the eggs, yoghurt, oil and ³/₄ cup (150g) brown sugar in a bowl until combined.

Add 180g berries to the flour mixture and stir to combine. Gently fold in the egg mixture until just combined. Spoon the mixture into the muffin holes and bake for 20 minutes or until a skewer inserted in the centre comes out clean.

Meanwhile, place the remaining berries and 50g brown sugar in a saucepan with 1 tablespoon water. Cook, stirring, over low heat for 2-3 minutes until the berries soften slightly. Set the berry syrup aside to cool slightly.

Dust the muffins with icing sugar and serve with the warm berry syrup.

Egyptian baked eggs

Serves 4

Bored with the same old eggs for breakfast on the weekend?
Try these spicy little numbers for something different.

40g unsalted butter, plus melted butter
   to grease
4 eggs
1 cup (280g) thick Greek-style yoghurt
1 garlic clove, crushed
1 tbs chopped mint leaves,
   plus whole leaves to garnish
1 tsp hot paprika
Toasted cumin seeds, to garnish
Toasted Turkish bread, to serve

Preheat the oven to 170°C and grease
4 ramekins or shallow ovenproof dishes
with melted butter.

Crack an egg into each ramekin and carefully
place the ramekins in a roasting pan. Pour
enough boiling water to come three-quarters
up the sides of the ramekins, then carefully
place the pan in the oven. Bake for 5-7 minutes
until the eggwhites are just set but the yolks
are still a little runny.

Meanwhile, mix the yoghurt, garlic and mint
in a bowl, season with salt and pepper and mix
well. Set aside. Melt the 40g butter with the
paprika in a frypan over medium-low heat.
Stir for 1 minute until fragrant.

Place the ramekins on serving plates
and drizzle with some of the paprika butter.
Sprinkle with cumin seeds, and garnish
with mint leaves. Serve with the yoghurt
and Turkish toast.

Son-in-law eggs

Serves 2

I first tasted these at Billy Kwong, my favourite Chinese restaurant in Sydney.
Once tried, never forgotten – thanks Kylie!

2 eggs
3 cups (750ml) vegetable oil
1 butter lettuce, outer leaves discarded,
    leaves separated
2 large vine-ripened tomatoes,
    quartered
1 spring onion, very thinly sliced
1 long red chilli, thinly sliced on an angle
Fried Asian shallots* and chopped
    toasted peanuts, to garnish
2 tbs oyster sauce

Break the eggs into 2 separate cups. Heat the oil in a wok or saucepan over high heat. Just before the oil starts to smoke, carefully slide the eggs, one at a time, into the oil and fry for 1 minute, basting and turning with a long metal spoon (be careful, as the oil will spit slightly), until the white is crisp and cooked – the yolk will still be a little runny.

Use a slotted spoon to remove the eggs from the oil, then place on paper towel to drain.

Place the lettuce leaves on 2 serving plates. Place an egg in each lettuce cup with some of the tomato. Top with the onion and chilli and garnish with fried shallots and peanuts. Drizzle over the oyster sauce.

* Fried Asian shallots are available from Asian food shops and selected supermarkets.

Anglo-Indian eggs

Serves 4

Okay, I know it's a bit naughty, but you don't have to use much of the sauce.
The hollandaise adds a delicious richness to the dish and makes it so easy.

8 eggs
1 tbs canola oil
1 large onion, thinly sliced
10-12 fresh curry leaves*
1 tbs panch phora*
2-3 tbs mild curry powder
200ml ready-made hollandaise sauce*
200ml pure (thin) cream
270ml can coconut milk
1/4 cup (60ml) lemon juice
Steamed basmati rice and naan bread,
   to serve
Coriander leaves, to garnish

Place the eggs in a saucepan and cover with plenty of cold water. Bring to the boil, then decrease the heat to medium and simmer for 6 minutes until hard-boiled. Refresh the eggs under cold water and peel when cool enough to handle. Halve the eggs and set aside.

Heat the oil in a heavy-based saucepan over medium heat. Add the onion and cook for 3-5 minutes until softened. Add the curry leaves and panch phora and cook, stirring, for 1 minute until fragrant. Stir in the curry powder and cook for a further 1 minute until fragrant. Add the hollandaise, cream and coconut milk and simmer over low heat for 2-3 minutes. Season with salt and pepper, then add the lemon juice and halved eggs and warm through gently.

Spoon the eggs and sauce onto the steamed rice, garnish with coriander leaves and serve with naan bread.
* Curry leaves are available from greengrocers and Indian food shops. Panch phora (a mix of whole spices including cumin, fennel, fenugreek, mustard and nigella seeds) is available from Indian and gourmet food shops. Hollandaise sauce is available from supermarkets.

Greek salad frittata

Serves 4

Leftover feta and olives in the fridge? A frittata is always a delicious, easy way to use up extra ingredients. It's great in lunchboxes the next day, too.

10 eggs
2 tbs chopped flat-leaf parsley
2 tbs olive oil
1 red onion, cut into thin wedges
1/2 punnet (125g) cherry tomatoes, halved
1/2 cup (80g) pitted kalamata olives
100g feta, cut into cubes

Preheat the oven to 180°C.

Lightly whisk the eggs and parsley in a bowl, then season with salt and pepper. Set aside.

Heat the oil in a 20cm ovenproof frypan over medium heat. Add the onion and cook for 2-3 minutes until softened. Add the tomato and olives and cook for a further 2 minutes until the tomato begins to soften. Pour over the egg mixture, scatter with the cheese and bake in the oven for 20 minutes until the egg has set.

Leave the frittata to stand in the pan for 10 minutes, then slice and serve warm or at room temperature.

Spaghetti with quail eggs and roasted garlic

Serves 4

1 whole garlic bulb
1 tbs olive oil, plus extra to drizzle
1 slice rustic-style woodfired bread
2 tbs grated parmesan
2 tbs flat-leaf parsley leaves
250g creme fraiche
400g spaghetti
12 quail eggs*
100g wild rocket leaves

Preheat the oven to 180°C.

Drizzle the garlic with 1 tablespoon of oil, wrap tightly in foil and place on a baking tray. Drizzle the bread on both sides with extra oil and place on the same tray. Bake, turning the bread once, for 15 minutes until the bread is golden. Remove the bread, then roast the garlic for a further 30 minutes until soft.

Meanwhile, pulse the bread, parmesan and parsley in a food processor to form coarse crumbs. Set aside.

Unwrap the roasted garlic. When cool enough to handle, squeeze the cloves from their skins into the creme fraiche. Mash together well and set aside.

Cook the spaghetti in boiling salted water according to packet instructions. Add the quail eggs for the last 4 minutes of cooking time, then drain. Remove the eggs and set aside. Toss the pasta in a little extra oil, then toss with the creme fraiche mixture and rocket. Season and divide among 4 bowls.

Peel the eggs (it helps to roll them on the bench first to ease off the shell), then halve and place on the pasta. Serve scattered with the parmesan crumbs.

* Available from selected poultry suppliers, delis and Asian food shops. Substitute 4 small hen's eggs, hard-boiled and quartered.

Heirloom tomato stacks with basil oil

Serves 4

Growers' markets are a great place to source wonderful heirloom tomatoes in the warmer months. It's hard to believe a dish so beautiful can have so few ingredients.

4-5 brightly coloured heirloom
    tomatoes* (such as oxheart,
    yellow, kumato and green zebra)
    or vine-ripened tomatoes
500g buffalo mozzarella or bocconcini

Basil oil
1/2 cup basil leaves, plus purple basil*
    leaves to garnish
1/3 cup (80ml) extra virgin olive oil

To make the basil oil, place the basil in a sieve and pour over boiling water. Refresh under cold water and drain well. Place the leaves in a small blender with the oil, season with salt and pepper and blend until smooth.

Cut the tomatoes crossways into 1cm slices, then season well with salt and pepper. Slice the mozzarella or bocconcini to the same thickness as the tomato.

Make stacks of layered tomato and cheese, drizzling the slices with basil oil as you go. Drizzle each plate with a little extra basil oil, then season with salt and pepper and serve garnished with purple basil leaves.

* Heirloom tomatoes and purple basil are from selected greengrocers and growers' markets. Use regular green basil in place of purple.

Oysters with homemade soda bread

Serves 6

This is a great way to show your guests that you care – homemade bread always hits the spot!

2 small eschalots, very finely chopped
100ml red wine vinegar
1 tsp caster sugar
1 tbs chopped flat-leaf parsley
36 freshly shucked oysters
Unsalted butter, to serve

Soda bread
3 cups (450g) plain flour
1 tsp caster sugar
1 tsp bicarbonate of soda
350ml buttermilk

For the soda bread, preheat the oven to 220°C. Grease and flour a baking tray.

Sift the flour into a large bowl, add the sugar, bicarbonate of soda and 1 teaspoon salt and mix well to combine. Make a well in the centre, then add the buttermilk and use your hands to bring together into a soft dough, kneading gently for 1 minute.

Tip the dough onto a floured surface and form into a 20cm round. Place on the prepared tray, score a cross in the top and dust lightly with extra flour. Bake for 15 minutes, then reduce the oven temperature to 190°C and bake for a further 30 minutes until the bread is golden and sounds hollow when tapped underneath. Place on a rack to cool slightly.

Meanwhile, combine the eschalot, vinegar, sugar and parsley in a bowl and season with salt and pepper. Spoon over the oysters and serve with the warm bread and butter.

Prosciutto & celeriac verrines

Makes 6

Verrines, both sweet and savoury, are taking Europe by storm. Simply choose your favourite serving glasses (*verres* in French), then artfully layer your ingredients.

1 small celeriac, peeled
1 Granny Smith apple
Juice of $^1/_2$ lemon
$^1/_2$ cup (150g) whole-egg mayonnaise
2 tsp Dijon mustard
2 tsp wholegrain mustard
100ml creme fraiche or sour cream
1 small red onion, thinly sliced
12 thin prosciutto slices
Watercress sprigs, to garnish
Balsamic glaze*, to serve

Using a mandoline slicer, cut the celeriac and apple into fine matchsticks (or use a sharp knife to slice very thinly, then cut into matchsticks). Toss in a bowl with the lemon juice to keep from browning.

In a separate bowl, combine the mayonnaise, mustard and creme fraiche or sour cream, season to taste with salt and pepper, then fold in the celeriac mixture and onion.

Divide the celeriac between 6 serving glasses. Curl 2 slices of prosciutto in each glass. Garnish with watercress and serve with the balsamic glaze to drizzle.
* Available from supermarkets.

Niçoise tarts

Makes 8

Any leftover tuna paté makes a great dip or sandwich spread.

2 sheets frozen puff pastry, thawed
225g can good-quality tuna in oil
30g unsalted butter, softened
1 tbs lemon zest
2 anchovy fillets
1 cup mache* or wild rocket leaves
16 cherry tomatoes, halved
24 niçoise olives* (or other small
    black olives)
16 quail eggs*, cooked in boiling
    water for 3-4 minutes, halved
Extra virgin olive oil, to drizzle

Preheat the oven to 180°C and line a tray with baking paper.

Cut four 8cm circles from each pastry sheet and place on the prepared tray. Cover with another sheet of baking paper and a second baking tray and bake for 10-12 minutes until crisp and golden. Set aside to cool.

Meanwhile, place the tuna, butter, lemon zest, anchovies and some freshly ground black pepper in a food processor and process until smooth.

Spread the tarts with some of the tuna paté, then garnish with the rocket, tomato, olives and quail eggs. Drizzle over the oil.

* Mache (lamb's lettuce) is available from selected greengrocers. Niçoise olives are available from delis and selected supermarkets. Quail eggs are available from selected poultry suppliers, delis and Asian food shops.

Pint of prawns with bacon mayo

Serves 4

Bacon-flavoured mayo may sound unusual, but you'll love its smoky flavour teamed with prawns – and it's pretty good on a steak sandwich, too.

6 bacon rashers
1 cup (300g) good-quality
   whole-egg mayonnaise
1 tbs chopped chives
Juice of 1 lemon,
   plus wedges to squeeze
1kg cooked tiger prawns

Cook the bacon in a non-stick frypan over medium heat for 8-10 minutes until crisp. Remove the bacon rashers and roughly chop, reserving the fat in the pan.

Place the chopped bacon, reserved fat, mayonnaise, chives and lemon juice in a food processor. Season with salt and pepper, then process until combined and the bacon is finely chopped.

Divide the prawns among pint mugs or large glasses and serve with the bacon mayo and lemon wedges to squeeze.

Chinese barbecue pork & snow pea salad

Serves 4

This is such an easy salad to put together. I love pea shoots with their crunchy tendrils, but if you can't find them add extra snow pea sprouts instead.

400g Chinese barbecue pork*,
    thinly sliced
100g snow peas, trimmed, blanched
2 cups pea shoots
150g snow pea sprouts, ends trimmed
3 spring onions, sliced on an angle
1 small red capsicum,
    cut into matchsticks
2 tbs toasted sesame seeds

Dressing
3 tsp rice vinegar
1 small red chilli, seeds removed,
    finely chopped
1/4 cup (60ml) light soy sauce
2cm piece ginger, cut into matchsticks
1/2 tsp sesame oil
1 star anise
2 tsp fresh lime juice

For the dressing, place the vinegar, chilli, soy sauce, ginger, sesame oil, star anise and lime juice in a small saucepan over low heat. Cook, stirring, for 2 minutes until warmed through. Remove from the heat and discard the star anise. Set aside to cool.

Combine the pork, snow peas, pea shoots, snow pea sprouts, onion and capsicum in a bowl. Toss with the dressing and transfer to a serving platter. Scatter with the sesame seeds.

* Available from Chinese restaurants and barbecue shops.

Goat's cheese, beetroot & praline salad

Serves 4

Chop Vienna almonds to make a quick praline and give a wonderful, sweet crunch to this salad. If you can't find them, use toasted almonds or pecans instead.

2 bunches baby beetroot (we used
  golden* and regular) or 850g can
  baby beets, drained, halved
150g picked watercress sprigs
250g soft goat's cheese, crumbled
100g Vienna almonds*,
  roughly chopped

Dressing
2 tbs white wine vinegar
1 tbs maple syrup
1/4 cup (60ml) extra virgin olive oil
1 tsp Dijon mustard

If using fresh beetroot, remove the leaves, leaving some stalk, and cook in boiling salted water for 25 minutes or until tender. Drain and refresh, then peel and halve.

Whisk all the dressing ingredients in a bowl and season with salt and pepper.

Lay the beetroot and watercress on a platter. Scatter over the goat's cheese. Drizzle with the dressing and scatter with chopped almonds.
* Golden beetroot is available from selected greengrocers and growers' markets. Vienna almonds are available from nut shops and selected greengrocers.

Tomato couscous & salami salad

Serves 4

Chargrilling the peperoni salami adds a nice touch to this salad,
but it's not absolutely necessary, especially if you're short on time.

1 cup (250ml) tomato juice
1 cup (200g) couscous
2 tbs olive oil, plus extra to brush
12 slices peperoni
1 tsp grated lemon zest,
   plus 2 tbs juice
$^1/_2$ tsp chilli flakes
100g wild rocket leaves
$^1/_3$ cup (50g) semi-dried tomatoes
   in oil, drained, finely chopped
120g bocconcini, cut into 2cm cubes

Place the tomato juice in a saucepan over medium heat and bring to just below boiling point, then remove from the heat. Add the couscous and 1 tablespoon of the oil, then season with salt and pepper. Cover with a tea towel and stand for 10 minutes.

Place a chargrill or frypan over high heat. Brush the salami with a little extra oil and cook for 30 seconds each side until starting to crisp. Drain on paper towel.

Combine the lemon zest and juice, chilli flakes and remaining 1 tablespoon oil in a bowl and season with salt and pepper.

Use a fork to fluff the couscous grains. Add the rocket leaves, tomato, bocconcini, peperoni and the dressing and toss to combine. Pile the salad onto a serving platter.

Vietnamese chicken salad

Serves 4-6

A mandoline is the quickest way to shred and slice all the vegetables for this Asian salad.

1 barbecued chicken, skin and
    bones discarded, meat shredded
    (to give 3 cups)
1 large carrot, cut into matchsticks
1/2 Chinese cabbage (wombok), shredded
1/2 red onion, thinly sliced
1 Lebanese cucumber, thinly sliced
    on an angle
1 long red chilli, seeds removed,
    cut into matchsticks
3 spring onions, thinly sliced
1/2 cup each Thai basil, mint
    and coriander leaves
1/3 cup (50g) chopped toasted
    peanuts (optional)

Dressing
1/4 cup (60ml) fish sauce
1/4 firmly packed cup (50g) brown sugar
1 long red chilli (remove seeds
    for less heat), finely chopped
2 tsp grated fresh ginger
1 small garlic clove, chopped
100ml fresh lime juice

For the dressing, place the fish sauce and sugar in a small saucepan over low heat and cook, stirring, for 1-2 minutes until combined and the sugar has dissolved. Place in a blender with the chilli, ginger and garlic and blend until smooth. Stir in the lime juice and season with salt and pepper.

Combine the chicken, carrot, cabbage, onion, cucumber, chilli and most of the spring onion and herbs. Pour over half the dressing, toss well and divide among serving bowls. Garnish with peanuts, if desired, and remaining spring onion and herbs. Drizzle over the remaining dressing to serve.

Panzanella salad

Serves 6

1/2 sourdough loaf, torn into
   2.5cm chunks (to give 5 cups)
100ml olive oil
1 bunch basil, leaves picked
1 garlic clove, finely chopped
2 tbs red wine vinegar
1 small red onion, thinly sliced
2 red capsicums, roasted (or use
   ready-roasted capsicum pieces),
   cut into strips
200g buffalo mozzarella* or bocconcini,
   torn into pieces
250g punnet cherry tomatoes
1 cup (150g) pitted kalamata olives

Preheat the oven to 180°C.

Toss the bread in 2 tablespoons of the oil. Place on a baking tray and bake for 15-20 minutes until golden.

Meanwhile, finely chop 1 cup of basil leaves, reserving the remaining leaves to garnish. Combine with the remaining oil, garlic and vinegar. Season with salt and pepper.

Combine the croutons and all the remaining ingredients in a bowl and toss well with the dressing. Transfer to a serving platter and garnish with the reserved basil. Set aside for 30 minutes to allow the flavours to develop.

* Available from delis and gourmet food shops.

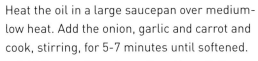

Spanish soup

Serves 4

This delicious soup works just as well chilled as it does hot, making it great for picnics and barbecues.

2 tbs olive oil
1 onion, chopped
2 garlic cloves, finely chopped
3 carrots (about 500g), peeled, chopped
1^1/$_2$ tsp ground cumin
1 tsp sweet paprika
400g can chopped tomatoes
2 cups (500ml) chicken stock
^{1}/$_4$ cup chopped flat-leaf parsley leaves
1 cup (250ml) dry sherry
Chopped hardboiled egg, curls of
    jamon* and small croutons, to serve

Heat the oil in a large saucepan over medium-low heat. Add the onion, garlic and carrot and cook, stirring, for 5-7 minutes until softened.

Add the cumin and paprika, stir well, then add the tomato and stock. Season with salt and pepper and bring to the boil. Reduce the heat to medium-low, partially cover and cook, stirring occasionally, for 18-20 minutes until the carrot is very tender.

Remove from the heat, then use a stick blender to puree the soup until smooth (or cool slightly, then puree in batches in a blender and return to the pan). Add the parsley and sherry, then warm through over low heat. Serve hot or chilled, garnished with egg, jamon and croutons, or serve the garnishes at the table in small bowls so everyone can help themselves.
* Jamon is Spanish cured ham, available from selected delis, or use prosciutto.

Pea & pea shoot soup with coriander and sweet chilli cream

Serves 4-6

2 tbs olive oil
20g unsalted butter
$1/2$ tsp ground cumin
2 tsp grated ginger
1 onion, finely chopped
1 potato, peeled, chopped
$1/2$ bunch coriander, stems cleaned
    and chopped, leaves picked
500g frozen peas
50g pea shoots*,
    plus extra to garnish
3 cups (750ml) chicken stock
2 tbs sweet chilli sauce
200ml creme fraiche or sour cream
Juice of 1 lemon

Heat the oil and butter in a large saucepan over low heat. Add the cumin and ginger and cook, stirring, for a few seconds until fragrant. Add the onion, potato and coriander stems and cook, stirring and adding a little water occasionally to prevent the vegetables from catching, for 5 minutes. Add the peas, pea shoots, stock and coriander leaves and bring to the boil. Decrease the heat to low and simmer for 3 minutes.

Meanwhile, swirl the sweet chilli sauce through the creme fraiche or sour cream.

Remove soup from the heat, then use a stick blender to puree the soup until smooth (or cool slightly, then puree in batches in a blender and return to the pan). Warm through over low heat, then season and stir in the lemon juice.

To serve, ladle the soup into bowls, swirl through some of the creme fraiche or sour cream, then garnish with pea shoots.
* Available from selected greengrocers. Substitute snow pea sprouts, stems trimmed.

Caesar salad soup

Serves 4-6

I love Caesar salad, so why not a Caesar salad soup? All the elements are here, plus a few peas for colour and potato for texture. And, as always, the anchovies are optional.

6 pancetta slices
1 tbs olive oil
1 onion, chopped
1 garlic clove, chopped
1-2 anchovy fillets, chopped (optional)
1 potato (about 200g), peeled, chopped
3 cups (750ml) chicken stock
200g frozen peas
1 cos lettuce, outer leaves discarded,
   thinly shredded
1/4 cup (20g) grated parmesan,
   plus extra to serve
2 tbs light sour cream
Toasted sourdough croutons, to serve

Preheat the oven to 200°C.

Lay 4 slices of pancetta on a baking tray, then cover with a sheet of baking paper and top with another tray to keep it flat. Place in the oven and bake for 10 minutes until crisp, then break into shards and set aside to serve.

Meanwhile, heat the oil in a saucepan over medium heat. Chop the remaining pancetta and add to the pan with the onion, garlic and anchovy and cook for 2-3 minutes until the onion has softened. Add the potato and stock and bring to the boil, then reduce the heat to medium-low, cover and simmer for 10 minutes until potato has softened.

Add the peas and lettuce and simmer for 2 minutes until the lettuce has wilted. Remove from the heat and cool slightly. Stir in the parmesan and season, then use a stick blender to puree the soup until smooth (or cool slightly, then puree in batches in a blender and return to the pan). Warm through over low heat or serve chilled. Divide among bowls, drizzle with sour cream, then serve with crisp pancetta shards, croutons and extra parmesan.

Thai-style tomato soup

Serves 4

5 ripe tomatoes (about 750g), quartered
1 onion, quartered
1 tbs olive oil, plus extra to drizzle
2 garlic cloves, chopped
1 tsp grated ginger
1 small red chilli, seeds removed,
   chopped, plus thinly sliced chilli
   to garnish
1 bunch coriander, stems cleaned
   and chopped, leaves picked
1/2 cup (125ml) tomato juice
270ml can coconut milk
1 tbs grated palm sugar*
   or brown sugar
2 tbs fish sauce
Fried Asian shallots*, to serve

Preheat the oven to 200°C.

Place the quartered tomato and onion on a lined baking tray, drizzle with a little oil and season with salt and pepper. Roast for 30 minutes until softened.

Heat the oil in a saucepan over medium heat. Add the garlic, ginger, chilli and coriander stems and cook, stirring, for 2-3 minutes until softened. Add tomato juice and coconut milk and bring to a simmer. Add the roasted tomato and onion with any pan juices, palm or brown sugar, fish sauce and coriander leaves (reserving some to garnish). Season and simmer over low heat for 10 minutes.

Remove from the heat, then use a stick blender to puree the soup until smooth (or cool slightly, then puree in batches in a blender and return to the pan). Warm through over low heat. Ladle into bowls and garnish with extra sliced chilli, reserved coriander leaves and fried Asian shallots.
* Palm sugar and fried Asian shallots are available from Asian food shops and selected supermarkets.

Mushroom soup with garlic bread

Serves 4-6

If you have any truffle oil in the pantry, drizzle a little over the soup just before serving for extra flavour and aroma.

1 tbs olive oil, plus extra to drizzle
50g unsalted butter
1 garlic clove, finely chopped
1 leek, thinly sliced
1 tbs chopped thyme leaves
400g Swiss brown mushrooms, chopped, plus 8 small whole mushrooms to serve (we used pine mushrooms)
10g dried porcini mushrooms*, soaked in $^1/_3$ cup (80ml) boiling water for 15 minutes
3 cups (750ml) chicken stock
2 tbs soy sauce
200ml thickened cream
Garlic bread (see Basics, p 246), to serve

Heat the oil and half the butter in a large saucepan over low heat. Add the garlic, leek and thyme and cook, stirring, for 3-5 minutes until the leek has softened. Add the chopped mushrooms, porcini and soaking liquid, stock and soy sauce and bring to the boil. Decrease heat to low and simmer for 5-8 minutes until the mushrooms have softened.

Remove from the heat, cool slightly, then puree using a stick blender (or puree in batches in a blender) until smooth. Return to a clean saucepan, add the cream and season with salt and pepper, then warm through over low heat.

Meanwhile, melt the remaining butter in a frypan over medium heat. Cook the small mushrooms, flat-side down, for 2-3 minutes until just softened. Season.

To serve, ladle soup into bowls, drizzle with extra oil and garnish with the pan-fried mushrooms. Serve with garlic bread.

* Dried porcini mushrooms are available from delis and selected greengrocers.

Instant fondue with roast vegetables

Serves 4-6

2 red capsicums
2 yellow capsicums
2 zucchini
1 small kumara (about 200g), peeled
6 garlic cloves (unpeeled)
2 tbs olive oil, plus extra to drizzle
12 thyme sprigs
300g wheel camembert or brie
Crusty bread, to serve

Preheat the oven to 190°C.

Cut the capsicum, zucchini and kumara into 2cm pieces. Place in a bowl with the garlic cloves and toss with the oil. Spread the vegetables in a baking dish and scatter with the thyme. Drizzle with a little more oil and bake, turning once, for 20-25 minutes until softened and just starting to brown.

Meanwhile, use a sharp knife to score a cross in the centre of the cheese rind. Place in the dish with the vegetables, then return to the oven for a further 5 minutes until the cheese starts to ooze and melt. Serve in the baking dish, with forks so everyone can dip their vegetables and crusty bread.

cheese

Baked polenta with four cheeses

Serves 6-8

This is a hearty winter dish and certainly feeds a crowd – a simple green salad makes
a refreshing accompaniment. Feel free to juggle the cheeses for a milder version.

400g instant polenta
3 cups (750ml) tomato passata (sugo)*
200g gorgonzola dolce*, chopped
250g Taleggio*, chopped
250g mascarpone cheese
100g freshly grated parmesan

Cook the polenta according to packet instructions, then pour into a greased, 5cm-deep, 23cm x 28cm baking dish. Stand for about 30 minutes until set.

Preheat the oven to 180°C.

Turn the set polenta out onto a cutting board and use a large serrated knife to carefully split it through the centre into two large slabs.

Pour half the tomato passata into the baking dish. Top with one of the slabs of polenta and season with salt and pepper. Scatter with the gorgonzola, Taleggio, mascarpone and half the parmesan. Top with the remaining polenta slab. Spread with the remaining passata and sprinkle with the remaining parmesan.

Bake for 30 minutes until bubbling and golden on top, then remove from the oven and stand for 10 minutes before serving.

* Tomato passata (sieved tomatoes) is available from supermarkets. Gorgonzola (a creamy blue cheese) and Taleggio (a washed rind cheese) are available from delis and gourmet food shops.

Figs with gorgonzola and prosciutto

Serves 6

6 fresh figs
100g gorgonzola dolce*, chopped
6 (about 100g) thin prosciutto slices
200ml thickened cream
Wild rocket leaves, to serve

Preheat the oven to 180°C and line a baking tray with baking paper.

Trim the fig stems and cut a small cross, about 2cm deep, in the top of each one. Gently squeeze the figs to open out slightly, then place a small piece of the gorgonzola in each cross. Wrap a slice of prosciutto around each fig then place on the tray and bake for 10 minutes until the cheese has melted.

Meanwhile, place the cream and remaining gorgonzola in a pan over low heat and whisk gently for 1-2 minutes until melted and smooth.

Drizzle the warm sauce over the figs, season with salt and pepper and serve with rocket.
* Gorgonzola is a creamy blue cheese available from delis and gourmet food shops.

Goat's cheese & quince jalousie

Serves 4-6

Sweetened goat's cheese makes a delicious filling for tarts and pies.

200g soft goat's cheese
2 tbs caster sugar
$1/2$ tsp vanilla extract
1 tbs finely grated lemon zest
375g block frozen puff pastry, thawed
200g quince paste*, chopped
1 egg, beaten
Icing sugar, to dust

Preheat the oven to 180°C and line a large baking tray with baking paper.

Place the goat's cheese, sugar, vanilla extract and lemon zest in a food processor and process until smooth.

On a lightly floured surface, roll the pastry to a large rectangle about 24cm x 38cm. Halve the pastry lengthways to make 2 long rectangles.

Place 1 rectangle on the lined tray and prick the base all over with a fork, leaving a 1cm border. Spread the base inside the border with the goat's cheese mixture, then scatter with the quince paste. Brush the pastry border with a little beaten egg.

Fold the other pastry rectangle in half lengthways and use a sharp knife to make cuts in the folded side about 2cm apart, leaving a 2cm border on the unfolded side. Carefully open the pastry back out and place over the filling, pressing to seal the edges – the cuts in the pastry should separate slightly to reveal some of the filling. Trim the edges if necessary, then brush all over with more beaten egg.

Bake for 25-30 minutes until puffed and golden, then stand for 10 minutes. Slice and serve warm, dusted with icing sugar.
* Quince paste is available from delis and selected supermarkets.

Strawberry & brie sandwiches

Makes 4

I know this combination sounds strange, but it really is delicious. I first tried it at a great little brunch place in Santa Monica, LA. Cut into fingers, they make great cocktail bites, too.

40g unsalted butter
8 slices brioche
50g strawberry jam
250g strawberries, hulled, sliced
175g chilled brie, sliced 1cm-thick
1-2 tbs caster sugar
Icing sugar, to dust

Use half the butter to spread on the brioche slices. Spread the unbuttered sides of 4 slices with jam, then cover with the strawberry slices and brie. Top with the remaining brioche, unbuttered-side down, then sprinkle the sandwiches all over with the caster sugar.

Melt the remaining butter in a frypan over medium heat. Add two sandwiches and cook for 1-2 minutes each side, pressing down gently with a spatula, until the bread is golden and the brie has melted. Keep warm while you cook the remaining sandwiches, then serve dusted with icing sugar.

DPS (daily pasta special)

Serves 4

When I had a gourmet food shop, this dish was so popular we couldn't take it off the menu (hence the name). It's the perfect pasta for when you want maximum flavour with minimum fuss.

2 tbs olive oil

4 garlic cloves, finely chopped

1 small red chilli, seeds removed,
   finely chopped

4 anchovy fillets, drained, chopped

20 basil leaves, chopped,
   plus extra leaves to garnish

1 cup (160g) pitted kalamata olives,
   chopped

2 tbs baby capers, rinsed

2 tbs tomato paste

600ml tomato passata (sugo)*

500g fettuccine

Grated parmesan,
   to serve (optional)

Heat the oil in a frypan over medium heat. Add the garlic, chilli, anchovy and basil and cook, stirring, for 1 minute or until fragrant. Add the olives, capers, tomato paste and passata and simmer, stirring occasionally, for 10 minutes until thickened.

Meanwhile, cook the pasta according to packet instructions. Drain, then divide among serving dishes. Spoon over the sauce, garnish with extra basil leaves and drizzle with extra virgin olive oil. Serve with parmesan, if desired.

* Available in bottles from supermarkets and greengrocers.

Rotelle with crushed peas, pancetta and mint

Serves 4

8 pancetta slices
250g vine-ripened cherry tomatoes
2 tbs olive oil, plus extra to toss
400g rotelle pasta
3 cups (360g) frozen peas
1/3 cup (80ml) pure (thin) cream
1 small bunch mint,
   leaves picked
1 cup (80g) grated parmesan

Preheat the oven to 180°C. Line 2 baking trays with baking paper.

Lay the pancetta slices on 1 tray. Place the tomatoes on the second tray, drizzle with the oil and season with salt and pepper. Place both trays in the oven (with the pancetta on top) and cook for 8-10 minutes until the pancetta is crisp and tomatoes begin to soften.

Meanwhile, cook the pasta according to packet instructions. Drain, then return to the pan, toss in a little oil and keep warm.

Cook the peas in boiling salted water for 3 minutes until tender, then drain.

Place 4 pancetta slices in a food processor with half the peas. Add the cream and half each of the mint and parmesan, then pulse briefly to crush – you want it to be quite coarse. Add the pea mixture to the pasta along with the remaining peas, then return the pan to low heat and toss for 1 minute to warm through.

Divide the pasta among bowls, tear over the remaining pancetta and top with roasted tomatoes, and remaining mint and parmesan.
* Rotelle are pasta wheels, available from delis and gourmet shops.

Prawn ravioli with sauce vierge

Serves 4

12 large green prawns, peeled,
   deveined
1 eggwhite
1 tbs thickened cream
1 tbs finely chopped chives
32 wonton wrappers*

Sauce vierge
90ml extra virgin olive oil
1 garlic clove, finely chopped
2 anchovy fillets, drained, chopped
   (optional)
2 vine-ripened tomatoes,
   seeds removed, finely chopped
Juice of $\frac{1}{2}$ lemon, plus wedges to serve
2 tbs finely chopped basil leaves
1 tbs finely chopped flat-leaf parsley

For the sauce vierge, place the oil, garlic and anchovy in a saucepan over low heat and cook, stirring, for 1 minute or until the anchovy has melted. Add the tomato and cook for a further minute until warmed through. Remove from the heat, stir in the lemon juice and season. Set aside while you make the ravioli.

Place 8 prawns in a food processor with the eggwhite, cream and chives. Season with salt and pepper, then pulse until combined. Quarter the remaining prawns.

Lay 16 wonton wrappers on the workbench. Place a heaped teaspoon of the prawn mixture on each and top with a piece of prawn. Brush the edges of the wonton wrapper with water, then top with a second wrapper, pressing the edges to seal and pushing out as much air as possible.

Cook the ravioli in a large pan of boiling salted water, in batches if necessary, for 2-3 minutes until they rise to the surface. Remove with a slotted spoon and divide among serving plates.

Meanwhile, return the sauce to low heat, add the herbs and stir to warm through gently.

Spoon the sauce vierge over the ravioli and serve with lemon wedges to squeeze.
* Available from Asian food shops and selected supermarkets.

Wild mushroom & truffle orzotto

Serves 4

The truffle butter is a real indulgence. If you can't find it, simply drizzle
with a little truffle oil before serving.

1 tbs olive oil
20g unsalted butter
500g mixed mushrooms
   (such as Swiss brown,
   button and flat mushrooms), sliced
1/2 cup (125ml) dry white wine
1 cup (250ml) chicken stock
400g orzo (risoni) pasta
2 tbs truffle butter* or truffle oil*
2 tbs chopped flat-leaf parsley
Grated parmesan or slices of
   ripe brie or Taleggio*, to serve

Heat the oil and butter in a large frypan
over high heat. Add the mushrooms and cook,
stirring occasionally, for 3 minutes or until
wilted and starting to brown. Reduce the
heat to medium, add the wine and simmer
for 2-3 minutes until all the wine is absorbed.
Add the stock and cook, stirring occasionally,
for 15 minutes or until most of the liquid
has been absorbed.

Meanwhile, cook the pasta in boiling salted
water according to packet instructions. Drain.

Stir the truffle butter or oil and parsley into
the mushroom mixture and season well with
sea salt and pepper. Add the pasta and stir well
to combine, then divide among bowls and serve
topped with parmesan, brie or Taleggio.
* Truffle butter, truffle oil and Taleggio
(an Italian washed rind cheese) are available
from gourmet food shops and delis.

Spaghetti with beetroot and marinated feta

Serves 4

Pink pasta – what next? The classic combination of beetroot
and feta works a treat in this easy supper dish.

450g can whole baby beetroot
2 tbs olive oil
1 onion, thinly sliced
2 garlic cloves, finely chopped
$\frac{1}{2}$ cup (125ml) port
2 tsp creamed horseradish
$\frac{1}{2}$ cup (125ml) vegetable stock
400g spaghetti
150g Persian (marinated) feta*,
   drained, crumbled
Chopped chives, to serve

Drain the beetroot, reserving the juice,
then cut into 2cm cubes.

Heat the oil in a frypan over medium
heat. Add the onion and cook, stirring, for
3-4 minutes until softened. Add the garlic
and cook, stirring, for a further minute,
then add the port, horseradish and stock.
Season with salt and pepper and simmer
for 2-3 minutes until the liquid has reduced.
Remove from the heat and stir in the beetroot.

Meanwhile, bring a large saucepan of salted
water to the boil with the reserved beetroot
juice. Cook the pasta in the flavoured water
according to packet instructions. Drain, then
toss with the sauce. Divide among bowls,
then serve scattered with feta and chives.
* A creamy feta available from delis
and selected supermarkets.

Spicy swordfish with avocado & lime salsa

Serves 4

1 lime, plus 2 tbs lime juice
  and wedges to serve
1 avocado, flesh cut into 1cm cubes
1 Lebanese cucumber, peeled,
  halved lengthways, seeds removed,
  cut into 1cm cubes
1/2 small red onion, finely chopped
1-2 long red chillies (to taste),
  seeds removed, finely chopped
1 cup coriander leaves
1/4 cup (60ml) olive oil, plus extra
  to brush and shallow-fry
2 tsp fish sauce
2 tbs plain flour
2 tsp each of ground coriander,
  cumin and paprika
1/2 tsp ground turmeric
4 x 180g swordfish or tuna steaks

Remove the skin and white pith from the lime. Holding the lime over a bowl to catch any juice, use a small sharp knife to cut the segments away from the inner membrane, then finely chop. Place chopped lime in a bowl with the avocado, cucumber, onion, chilli and coriander. Combine the oil, fish sauce and lime juice in a small bowl, then toss with the salsa. Set aside.

Combine the flour and dry spices in a shallow dish. Brush the fish with a little extra oil, then dip in the seasoned flour to coat, shaking off the excess.

Heat 2cm of olive oil in a large frypan over medium heat. Cook the fish, in batches if necessary, for 2-3 minutes each side until browned but still a little rare in the centre.

Serve the fish topped with the avocado salsa, with extra lime wedges to squeeze.

My fish curry

Serves 4

If you want the heat and spice of a curry but don't
have time for slow-cooking, fish is a speedy option.

2 tbs sunflower oil
1 tsp yellow mustard seeds
1 onion, sliced
1 cinnamon quill
3cm piece ginger, grated
4 garlic cloves, thinly sliced
1 long red chilli, seeds removed,
   thinly sliced
1 tsp ground cumin
2 tsp ground coriander
1/2 tsp ground turmeric
1/2 tsp garam masala spice blend
12 fresh curry leaves*
2 tomatoes, seeds removed,
   cut into thin wedges
300ml fish or chicken stock
400ml coconut milk
450g boneless, skinless firm white
   fish fillets (such as blue-eye),
   cut into 3cm cubes
Coriander leaves, to garnish
Steamed basmati rice, pappadams and
   tomato kasundi or chutney, to serve

Heat the oil in a deep frypan over medium heat.
Add the mustard seeds and cook for 1 minute
or until they start to pop. Add the onion,
cinnamon and 1 teaspoon salt and cook,
stirring occasionally, for 2-3 minutes until
onion has softened. Add the ginger, garlic,
chilli, dry spices, curry leaves, tomato and
1/2 cup (125ml) stock and cook for 3-4 minutes
until nearly all the liquid has evaporated.

Add the coconut milk and remaining
stock and simmer over medium heat for
5 minutes. Add the fish and simmer for a
further 5 minutes or until the fish is cooked
through. Season with salt and pepper.

Garnish with coriander and serve with
steamed basmati rice, pappadams and
tomato kasundi or chutney.
* Available from selected greengrocers
and Asian food shops.

Moroccan-style fish with chermoula

Serves 4

Chermoula is an aromatic North African spice paste that's fantastic with fish. It's quite readily available now, but the heat level can vary so feel free to add a little more or less to taste.

¼ cup (60ml) vegetable oil
1 onion, thinly sliced
2 tbs chermoula paste*
4 tomatoes, seeds removed,
  cut into wedges
600ml fish stock
¼ preserved lemon*, flesh and white
  pith discarded, skin thinly sliced
8 small chat potatoes, cut into wedges
4 x 150g firm white fish cutlets
  or fillets (such as jewfish)
16 niçoise or other small black olives
1 tbs chopped coriander leaves
2 tbs chopped mint, plus extra
  mint leaves to garnish
Couscous, to serve

Heat half the oil in a frypan over medium heat. Add the onion and cook, stirring occasionally, for 3-4 minutes until softened. Add the chermoula paste, tomato, stock and half the preserved lemon, then bring to the boil. Decrease the heat to low and simmer for 20 minutes until slightly thickened. Add the potato and simmer for 6 minutes until tender.

Meanwhile, heat the remaining oil in a frypan over medium-high heat. Season the fillets with salt and pepper, then cook for 2-3 minutes each side until almost cooked through.

Add the fish to the sauce with the remaining preserved lemon, olives, coriander and mint. Warm through, then garnish with extra mint and serve with couscous.

* Preserved lemon and chermoula (a North African herb and spice paste, see Glossary) are available from delis and gourmet shops.

Blue-eye with Spanish crumbs

Serves 4

The smoky, flavoursome crumbs work so well with firm white fish. I like
to serve this with potatoes that have been pan-fried with chorizo sausage.

2 anchovy fillets, drained
1 tbs capers, rinsed
Zest of 1 lemon
1/4 cup (60ml) olive oil,
  plus extra to drizzle
1 tsp Spanish smoked paprika
  (pimenton)*
2 tbs chopped flat-leaf parsley
1 tbs toasted pine nuts
100g sourdough bread, crust removed
4 x 180g skinless blue-eye fillets,
  pin-boned
2 bunches asparagus, trimmed
250g cherry truss tomatoes
Aioli (garlic mayonnaise) and
  pan-fried potatoes with chorizo
  (optional, see Basics p 246), to serve

Preheat the oven to 200°C.

Place the anchovies, capers, lemon zest,
oil, paprika, parsley and pine nuts in a food
processor and process to a paste. Add the
bread and process to coarse crumbs (adding
a little more oil if needed, to keep the mixture
moist). Sprinkle 3 tablespoons of the crumb
mixture on a baking tray and set aside.

Season the fish with salt and pepper,
then place in a lined roasting pan. Divide the
remaining crumb mixture among each fish
fillet to cover, pressing in gently to form a
crust. Spread asparagus and tomatoes around,
drizzle with extra oil and season. Place the fish
on the top shelf of the oven, and the tray with
remaining crumbs on the bottom shelf. Bake
for 10 minutes or until the fish is cooked
through and the crumbs are golden.

Divide fish and vegetables among serving
plates, scatter with extra crumbs and serve
with aioli, potatoes and chorizo if desired.
* Available from delis and gourmet shops.

Baja fish tacos

Serves 6

These wonderful fish tacos are sold all along the coast in Baja, Mexico. The pico de gallo is a spicy relish that makes them extra special. Serve with lots of lime and cold Mexican beer.

1/2 tsp each of ground coriander,
    cumin, turmeric and chilli powder
1/2 cup (75g) plain flour
6 x 180g skinless flathead fillets
1/4 cup (60ml) olive oil
12 small flour tortillas,
    warmed to packet instructions
1/2 iceberg lettuce, thinly shredded
1/2 red onion, thinly sliced
1 tomato, seeds removed, thinly sliced
Pico de gallo (see Basics, p 246),
    to serve
Sour cream, coriander leaves
    and lime wedges, to serve

Combine the dry spices and flour in a shallow dish and season with salt and pepper. Toss the fish fillets in the seasoned flour, shaking off any excess.

Heat the oil in a frypan over medium-low heat. Fry the fish, in batches, for 2-3 minutes on each side until golden and cooked through. Keep warm while you cook the remaining fish.

Slice the fish into long strips and place in the warm tortillas with the lettuce, onion, tomato, some pico de gallo, sour cream and coriander leaves. Serve with lime wedges to squeeze.

Baked whole salmon with wasabi tartare

Serves 10-12

This is a great way to feed a crowd, and if you don't manage to eat it all on the day, it's just as good cold the next. Serve with parsley potatoes and a green salad.

2 eggs
1 garlic clove
1/2 tsp wasabi paste
Zest and juice of 1 lime,
    plus 1 lime sliced
2/3 cup (165ml) light olive oil
2 tbs baby capers, rinsed
8 cornichons (small pickled
    cucumbers), roughly chopped
1/2 bunch coriander,
    leaves roughly chopped
1 small whole salmon or ocean trout*
    (about 2kg), filleted, skin removed,
    pin-boned
200g creme fraiche
2 cups mixed baby herb
    and salad leaves

Pulse the eggs, garlic, wasabi and lime zest in a food processor. Season with salt and pepper. With the motor running, add oil in a slow steady stream until you have a thick sauce. Add capers, cornichons, coriander and 1 tablespoon of lime juice (or more to taste), then pulse to combine.

Preheat the oven to 180°C.

Line a large baking tray with baking paper. Place a fillet on the tray, skinned-side down. Spread with half the sauce (reserving the rest to serve), then lay the lime slices down the length of the fillet. Top with the remaining fillet, skinned-side up. Cover with a sheet of baking paper, then enclose the fish completely in foil. Bake for 45 minutes, then remove and stand, still wrapped in foil, for a further 10 minutes to finish cooking. Test to see if the fish is cooked by gently pressing at the thickest part of the flesh – it should flake easily (cover with foil for a little longer if needed). Remove the foil and paper and carefully slide the salmon onto a serving platter. Stand for 15 minutes to cool to room temperature, or refrigerate until ready to serve.

Fold the creme fraiche into the reserved sauce. Scatter the fish with herb and salad leaves, then serve with the sauce.

* Order from fishmongers and ask them to fillet the salmon for you.

Smoked salmon & cream cheese terrine

Serves 6 as a starter

This dish has a touch of the '70s about it, but it's great as a summer starter or for picnics. I used a small terrine, but you could double the quantities and use a 1-litre loaf pan.

350g cream cheese
300ml thickened cream
Zest of 1 lemon, plus wedges to serve
Pinch cayenne pepper
12 large smoked salmon slices
Olive oil, to drizzle
Chervil or flat-leaf parsley sprigs,
   to garnish
Toasted baguette, to serve

Line a 6cm-deep, 18cm x 7cm rectangular terrine mould or loaf pan with plastic wrap, leaving plenty overhanging the sides.

Place the cream cheese, cream, lemon zest and cayenne in a food processor and process until smooth.

Cover the base and sides of the terrine with salmon, leaving enough overhanging to cover the top. Spread the base with a 1cm-thick layer of the cheese mixture, then cover with more salmon, cutting slices to fit if necessary. Continue to layer the cheese mixture and salmon, then fold in the overhanging salmon and cover with any remaining slices. Cover the top with plastic wrap, pressing down well, and chill for 2-3 hours to firm up.

When ready to serve, turn out the terrine and slice using a knife dipped in hot water. Place on a platter, drizzle with oil and garnish with chervil or parsley. Serve with lemon wedges and toasted baguette.

Salmon with tomato & coconut sambal

Serves 4

¼ cup (60ml) sunflower oil
2 Asian red eschalots*, thinly sliced
2 long green chillies, seeds removed,
  finely chopped
2cm piece ginger, grated
1 garlic clove, thinly sliced
2 tsp mild curry powder
10 fresh curry leaves*
250g cherry tomatoes, halved
270ml can coconut cream
Juice of 2 limes
4 salmon cutlets
Steamed rice, to serve
Coriander leaves, to garnish

Heat 2 tablespoons of the oil in a wok or saucepan over low heat. Add the eschalot, chilli, ginger and garlic and cook for 4-6 minutes until softened.

Add the curry powder, curry leaves and tomato, half the coconut cream and 2 tablespoons water and cook for 2-3 minutes until the tomato has started to break down slightly. Stir in the remaining coconut cream and lime juice, season to taste and simmer for 5 minutes until thickened slightly.

Meanwhile, heat the remaining oil in a frypan over medium-high heat. Season the salmon and cook for 2-3 minutes each side (or until cooked to your liking), then add to the sauce. Serve with rice, garnished with coriander.

* Asian red eschalots are available from Asian food shops. Fresh curry leaves are available from selected greengrocers.

Salmon baklava with dill butter

Serves 4

These are great as a starter or light lunch, or make a smaller version for cocktail food.

8 sheets filo pastry, thawed if necessary
125g unsalted butter, melted
4 x 150g skinless salmon fillets,
  pin-boned
2 garlic cloves, finely chopped
1 tbs chopped dill
Zest strips and juice of 1 lemon

Preheat the oven to 190°C. Line a baking tray with baking paper.

Make 2 stacks of 4 filo sheets each, brushing between each layer with some melted butter (and keeping unused pastry covered with a clean tea towel while you work to prevent it from drying out). Cut each filo stack in half.

Place a salmon fillet on 1 filo stack and season well. Fold over 1 end of the pastry, then fold in the sides and roll up to enclose. Place seam-side down on the tray, then repeat with the remaining salmon and pastry. Brush the parcels with a little more butter, then bake for 20 minutes until golden.

Meanwhile, place the remaining butter, garlic, dill, lemon zest and juice in a small saucepan over low heat and stir until warmed through. Serve the salmon parcels drizzled with the dill butter.

Teriyaki salmon with wasabi & avocado sauce

Serves 4

4 x 180g skinless salmon fillets
100ml soy sauce
100ml mirin (Japanese rice wine)*
Juice of 1 lemon
3 tsp wasabi paste*, or to taste
2 avocados, flesh chopped
1 tbs sunflower oil
Japanese pickled ginger*
  and lime wedges, to serve

Place the salmon fillets in a snap-lock bag. Combine the soy and mirin in a bowl and place ¼ cup (60ml) of the mixture in the bag with the salmon, seal and marinate in the fridge for up to a day ahead.

Combine half the lemon juice with the remaining soy mixture. Place in dipping bowls.

Place the wasabi, avocado and remaining lemon juice in a food processor. Process until smooth and season to taste.

Heat a large non-stick frypan over medium heat. Remove the salmon from the bag, reserving any remaining marinade, then rub with the oil. Cook for 2-3 minutes each side until cooked but still a little rare in the centre. Add the reserved marinade and allow to bubble for 1 minute.

Serve with wasabi and avocado sauce, soy dipping sauce, pickled ginger and lime wedges.
* Available from selected supermarkets and Asian food shops.

Thai lobster curry

Serves 2

Lobster gives this dish a touch of luxury, but prawns, crab or bug tails work well, too.

1 green lobster*
400ml coconut milk
400ml chicken stock
1 lemongrass stem (pale part only),
   halved
3 kaffir lime leaves
3-4 tbs Thai green curry paste (to taste)
3 tsp fish sauce
3 tsp caster sugar
$1/2$ cup (60g) frozen peas
2-3 tbs lime juice
1 cup bean sprouts, trimmed
1 cup Thai basil leaves
1 cup coriander leaves
1 long red chilli, thinly sliced
Lime wedges and steamed
   jasmine rice, to serve

Place the lobster in the freezer for 20 minutes to put it to sleep. Bring a large saucepan of salted water to the boil and add the lobster. Bring back to the boil, then reduce the heat to low. Add the lobster, return to the boil and simmer for 15-20 minutes until the shell turns deep red. Drain, then set aside to cool slightly.

Meanwhile, place the coconut milk, stock, lemongrass and kaffir lime leaves in a pan over medium heat and bring to the boil. Add the curry paste, fish sauce and sugar to taste, decrease heat to low and simmer for 5 minutes.

Cut the lobster in half and clean, leaving only the meat in the shell. Add lobster halves to the sauce with the peas and simmer for 2 minutes, then stir in lime juice to taste.

Ladle into bowls and top with bean sprouts, Thai basil, coriander and chilli. Serve with lime wedges and jasmine rice.

* Available from selected fishmongers.

Scallops with lentils and chorizo

Serves 4

2 tbs olive oil
1 onion, finely chopped
1 chorizo sausage, skin removed,
  finely chopped
2 tsp harissa paste*
400g can chopped tomatoes
400g can lentils, rinsed, drained
16 scallops in the half shell
  (without roe)
Chopped flat-leaf parsley, to sprinkle
Baby basil, to garnish (optional)

Preheat the oven to 120°C.

Heat 1 tablespoon of the oil in a saucepan over medium heat. Add the onion and chorizo and cook for 5 minutes until the chorizo starts to crisp. Add the harissa, tomato and lentils and simmer for 5 minutes until thickened and very little liquid remains. Season with salt.

Meanwhile, warm the scallop shells on a baking tray in the oven for a few minutes. Place on a serving platter.

Heat the remaining 1 tablespoon oil in a frypan over high heat. Season the scallops with salt and pepper. In 2 batches, sear the scallops for 30 seconds on each side until golden but still opaque.

Divide the lentil mixture among the shells and top with the scallops. Sprinkle with the parsley and garnish with baby basil, if desired.
* Harissa is a North African chilli paste available from Middle Eastern and gourmet food shops (see Glossary).

Spicy crab tarts

Makes 8

2 large (quiche size) frozen shortcrust
   pastry sheets, thawed
200ml pure (thin) cream
1 egg, plus 1 extra yolk
1 long red chilli, seeds removed,
   finely chopped
2 tsp grated ginger
200g fresh crabmeat*, drained
2 spring onions, thinly sliced
2 tbs chopped coriander leaves
Baby herb salad and chilli oil*
   (optional), to serve

Preheat the oven to 180°C and grease eight 10cm loose-bottomed tart pans.

Use a 12cm cutter to cut 4 rounds from each pastry sheet, then use to line the tart pans. Chill for 10 minutes.

Line the pastry with baking paper and fill with pastry weights or uncooked rice. Place the pans on a tray and bake for 8 minutes. Remove the paper and pastry weights or rice, then bake the tart shells for a further 3 minutes until light golden.

Meanwhile, whisk the cream and egg in a bowl. Add the chilli and ginger, season with salt and pepper and mix well to combine.

Divide the crabmeat, spring onion and coriander among the tart shells. Pour over the egg mixture. Bake for 15 minutes or until the filling is just set. Serve with herb salad and a drizzle of chilli oil if desired.
* Fresh crabmeat is available from fishmongers. Chilli oil is available from Asian and gourmet food shops.

Prawn cakes on lemongrass skewers

Makes 10

The lemongrass skewers add a citrussy note to these prawn cakes, but for
a faster version you can leave them out and cook them like regular Thai fishcakes.

2 eschalots, finely chopped
2 tbs Thai green curry paste
   (or to taste)
1 small red chilli, seeds removed,
   finely chopped
1 tsp grated ginger
2 tsp fish sauce
1 tbs light soy sauce
1/4 cup chopped coriander leaves
300g skinless, boneless white fish
   fillets (such as ling)
200g green prawn meat
1 eggwhite
2 tbs plain flour
5 lemongrass stems, cut into
   ten 15cm pieces
Sunflower oil, to shallow-fry
Green papaya salad (see Basics, p 246),
   to serve
Lime wedges, to serve

Place the eschalot, curry paste, chilli, ginger,
fish sauce, soy sauce and coriander in a food
processor and pulse until combined. Add the
fish, prawn meat, eggwhite and flour, season
with salt and pepper and pulse until the
mixture comes together.

Using damp hands, roll the mixture into
10 small cakes. Use your hand to flatten
slightly, then mould each cake around a
lemongrass piece. Chill in the fridge to firm up.

Heat 3-4cm of sunflower oil in a frypan over
medium-low heat. Cook the prawn cakes, in
batches, for 2 minutes each side until golden.
Drain on paper towel. Serve with the green
papaya salad and lime wedges.

Salt-and-pepper squid and chips

Serves 4

I love salt-and-pepper squid, so why not add the same flavours to the chips, too?

1 tbs dried chilli flakes
1 tbs whole black peppercorns
1 tbs whole Szechuan peppercorns*
3/4 cup (100g) rice flour
1kg small squid
Peanut oil, to deep-fry
3 large potatoes (about 800g),
   peeled, cut into matchsticks
   (a mandoline is ideal for this)
Lime wedges and aioli*
   (garlic mayonnaise), to serve

Preheat the oven to 160°C.

Dry-roast the chilli, peppercorns and Szechuan pepper with 2 tablespoons of sea salt in a wok over medium heat for 2-3 minutes until fragrant. Grind to a powder in a spice grinder or mortar and pestle. Place in a bowl with the flour and mix well. Set aside.

Cut the tentacles away from the squid tubes, discarding beak. Open out the tubes and clean, then lightly score the insides of the tubes in a criss-cross pattern. Cut into bite-sized pieces.

Half-fill a wok or deep-fryer with oil and heat to 160°C. Fry the chips in the oil for 2 minutes until almost cooked, then remove and drain on paper towel. Toss the chips in half the flour mixture and set aside.

Increase oil to 190°C. Toss the squid tubes and tentacles in remaining flour mixture and shake off excess. Fry, in batches, for 2 minutes until crisp and golden. Drain well and keep warm in the oven while you finish the chips. Return the chips to the oil for a further 1-2 minutes until crisp and golden, then drain well.

Serve the salt-and-pepper squid and chips with lime wedges and aioli.

* Szechuan peppercorns are available from Asian food shops. Aioli is available from selected supermarkets and delis.

Vegetarian chilli in avocado

Serves 4

2 tbs olive oil
1 large onion, finely chopped
1 tsp dried chilli flakes
1/2 tsp ground cinnamon
1 tsp ground cumin
1 tsp dried thyme
2 garlic cloves, chopped
1 tbs tomato paste
420g can three-bean mix, rinsed, drained
400g can brown lentils, rinsed, drained
400g can chopped tomatoes
1/2 cup (125ml) vegetable stock
2 tbs chopped coriander leaves,
    plus extra leaves to garnish
Steamed rice, sour cream and
    corn chips, to serve
2 avocados, peeled, halved,
    stones discarded

Heat the oil in a large frypan over medium heat. Add the onion and cook, stirring, for 2-3 minutes until softened. Add the dry spices, thyme and garlic and cook for 30 seconds or until fragrant. Add the tomato paste and cook for a few seconds, then add the beans, lentils, tomato and stock and bring to a simmer. Decrease the heat to low, then simmer for 15 minutes or until the sauce has thickened. Remove from the heat and stir in the chopped coriander.

Divide the steamed rice among 4 serving bowls, place an avocado half in each. Top with the chilli, sour cream, black pepper and extra coriander. Serve with corn chips.

Kumara galettes

Makes 4

I first tasted a version of these delicious little pastries at Ottolenghi, the great Notting Hill deli in London. You can use pumpkin or parsnip instead of kumara.

2 small kumara, peeled, sliced into
  1cm-thick rounds
1 tbs olive oil, plus extra to brush
375g block frozen puff pastry or
  1 sheet frozen puff pastry, thawed
100ml creme fraiche or sour cream
100g Persian (marinated) feta*, drained
1 egg, lightly beaten
1 garlic clove, finely chopped
1 long red chilli, seeds removed,
  finely chopped
2 tbs chopped coriander leaves

Preheat the oven to 200°C. Line 2 baking trays with baking paper.

Place kumara in a single layer on 1 baking tray. Brush with oil and season with salt and pepper. Bake for 10-15 minutes until tender.

Meanwhile, if using a block of pastry, roll out on a lightly floured surface to a 24cm x 24cm square. Cut the rolled pastry or pastry sheet into four 12cm squares. Prick in several places with a fork, leaving a 2cm border. Place on the second baking tray and chill for 10 minutes.

Spread the pastries with creme fraiche or sour cream inside the border and season with salt and pepper. Top with the roasted kumara, slightly overlapping, and crumble over the feta. Brush the pastry edges with egg. Bake for 25 minutes or until golden and puffed.

Meanwhile, combine the oil, garlic, chilli and coriander in a small bowl and season with salt and pepper. As soon as the pastries come out of the oven, brush with some of the dressing. Serve the remaining dressing on the side.
* Persian feta is available from delis and selected supermarkets.

Risotto-stuffed tomatoes

Serves 4 as a main or 8 as a starter

8 large vine-ripened tomatoes
1 cup (220g) arborio rice
60g unsalted butter, chopped
1 small onion, finely chopped
2 tbs chopped thyme leaves
Grated zest of 2 lemons
1/4 cup (60ml) thickened cream
100g gruyere cheese, grated
Olive oil, to drizzle

Cut a small lid from each tomato. Using a teaspoon, scoop out and reserve the pulp and seeds. Place the tomatoes upside down on paper towel to drain.

Cook the rice in boiling salted water for 12 minutes until just beginning to soften. Drain.

Meanwhile, melt the butter in a frypan over medium heat. Add the onion and cook, stirring, for 2-3 minutes until softened. Add reserved tomato pulp and cook, stirring, for a further 1-2 minutes. Add the onion mixture to the rice with the thyme, lemon zest, cream and cheese, then season with salt and pepper.

Fill the tomatoes with the rice mixture, replace the lids, then place in a snug-fitting baking dish and drizzle with oil. Bake for 25-30 minutes until the tomatoes start to soften and rice is cooked through, then serve.

White bean & coconut curry

Serves 4

2 tbs sunflower oil
1 tsp yellow mustard seeds
12 fresh curry leaves*
1 onion, thinly sliced
2cm piece ginger, grated
4 garlic cloves, finely chopped
3 tsp mild curry powder
4 cardamom pods, lightly bruised
1/2 tsp ground turmeric
1/2 tsp chilli powder
1 tsp ground coriander
2/3 cup (165ml) coconut milk
2 x 400g cans cannellini beans,
  rinsed, drained
250g punnet cherry or grape tomatoes,
  halved
2 tsp sugar
Juice of 1 lime
2 tbs chopped coriander leaves,
  plus extra leaves to garnish
Basmati rice and naan bread, to serve

Heat the oil in a large saucepan over medium-low heat. Add the mustard seeds and cook for 30 seconds or until they start to pop. Add the curry leaves and onion and cook, stirring, for 3-5 minutes until the onion has softened.

Add the ginger, garlic, curry powder, cardamom and dry spices and cook, stirring, for 1-2 minutes until fragrant. Add the coconut milk and 200ml water and bring to a simmer. Reduce heat to low and simmer for 3-5 minutes until slightly thickened. Add the beans, tomato, sugar and lime juice and simmer for a further 2-3 minutes until the tomato has softened slightly. Stir through the chopped coriander leaves. Serve with rice and naan, garnished with extra coriander leaves.

* Available from selected greengrocers.

Baked gnocchi with Taleggio, gorgonzola and figs

Serves 4

700g potato gnocchi
150g gorgonzola dolce cheese*,
   chopped
100g Taleggio cheese*, chopped
200ml creme fraiche or sour cream
4 fresh figs, chopped
1/2 cup (40g) grated parmesan

Preheat the oven to 180°C. Grease
a 25cm x 20cm baking dish.
   Cook the gnocchi in boiling salted water
according to packet instructions. Drain well.
   Place the gnocchi, cheese, creme fraiche
or sour cream and figs in the baking dish,
season with black pepper and mix gently to
combine. Scatter with the parmesan. Bake
for 15-20 minutes until golden and bubbling.
* Gorgonzola (a creamy blue cheese) and
Taleggio (a washed rind cheese) are available
from delis and gourmet food shops.

Roast chicken with pan-roasted romesco

Serves 4

Romesco is a simple, classic Spanish sauce that's fantastic with poultry and fish.
Here it's made even easier by roasting the capsicum and tomato along with the chicken.

1/3 cup (80ml) olive oil
1 tbs smoked paprika (pimenton)*
1 tbs chopped rosemary leaves
8 garlic cloves
1.8kg free-range chicken
1 red capsicum, cut into chunks
1 tomato, cut into chunks
1/2 cup (80g) blanched almonds, toasted
1/4 cup (15g) fresh breadcrumbs,
    lightly oven-toasted
1/4 cup chopped flat-leaf parsley
1 cup (250ml) dry sherry

Combine 2 tablespoons of the oil, paprika, rosemary and 2 crushed garlic cloves in a bowl. Season, then rub mixture over the chicken. Cover and marinate in the fridge for 30 minutes.

Preheat the oven to 180°C.

Place the chicken in a roasting pan and roast for 1 hour. Scatter capsicum, tomato and remaining garlic cloves around the chicken and drizzle with remaining oil. Roast for a further 20 minutes or until the chicken is golden and cooked (the juices run clear when the thigh is pierced) and vegetables have softened.

Meanwhile, place the almonds, breadcrumbs and parsley in a food processor. Season and process until combined. Set aside.

Remove the chicken to a plate, cover loosely with foil and leave to rest while you finish the sauce. Place the roasting pan with vegetables over medium heat, add the sherry and cook, stirring, for 5 minutes until slightly reduced. Cool slightly, then place in a food processor with half the crumb mixture and process until smooth. Season with salt and pepper.

Serve the roast chicken on a platter or board sprinkled with the remaining crumb mixture, with the romesco sauce on the side.

* Available from delis and gourmet shops.

Oven-baked Thai chicken curry

Serves 4-6

1 tbs sunflower oil

1 onion, finely chopped

2 large (180-200g) free-range chicken
   breast fillets, cut into 2cm pieces

4 tbs Thai green curry paste
   (or to taste)

1¼ cups (250g) jasmine rice

Zest and juice of 1 lime

400ml coconut milk

1 lemongrass stem, bruised

3 kaffir lime leaves*, finely shredded

250g cherry tomatoes, halved if large

1 long red chilli, seeds removed, sliced

Coriander sprigs, Thai basil leaves*,
   fried Asian shallots* and creme
   fraiche or sour cream, to serve

Preheat the oven to 200°C.

Heat the oil in a wide flameproof casserole over medium heat. Add the onion and cook for 1-2 minutes until slightly softened. Add the chicken and curry paste, then cook, stirring, for 3-5 minutes until the chicken is just starting to brown and the paste is fragrant.

Add the rice, lime zest and juice, coconut milk, lemongrass, kaffir lime leaf (reserving a little to garnish) and 1 cup (250ml) water. Bring to the boil, then cover and bake in the oven for 15 minutes or until the chicken is cooked and the rice is tender, adding tomatoes for the final 5 minutes of cooking time.

Stand, covered, for 5 minutes, then stir well and serve in bowls topped with sliced chilli, herbs, fried shallots and a dollop of creme fraiche or sour cream.

* Available from Asian food shops and selected greengrocers.

Chicken schnitzel with avocado and pink grapefruit

Serves 4

I think it was at Bill Granger's eponymous restaurant that I first tasted
a chicken and pink grapefruit salad – it is such a great combination.

4 cups (280g) fresh breadcrumbs
1/2 cup (40g) grated parmesan
1 tbs chopped thyme leaves
4 tbs chopped flat-leaf parsley
1/2 cup (75g) plain flour
2 eggs, lightly beaten
4 x 150g chicken breast fillets,
  flattened slightly
2 ruby grapefruits
2 avocados, flesh sliced
1 baby cos or butter lettuce,
  leaves separated
2 tsp Dijon mustard
2 tsp white wine vinegar
1/3 cup (80ml) extra virgin olive oil
Sunflower oil, to shallow-fry
Chopped chives, to sprinkle

Place the breadcrumbs, parmesan, thyme
and parsley in a shallow bowl. Season with
salt and pepper and combine well.

Place the flour and egg in separate dishes.
Dip the chicken fillets firstly into the flour,
shaking off excess, then into egg and finally
in breadcrumb mixture, pressing to adhere.
Chill in the fridge for about 10 minutes while
you make the salad.

Meanwhile, peel the grapefruit and remove
the pith, then slice the flesh into segments
over a bowl to catch any juices. Arrange the
grapefruit segments, avocado and lettuce
on serving plates.

Whisk together the mustard, vinegar and
olive oil in a bowl with 1-2 tablespoons of the
reserved grapefruit juice to taste. Season with
salt and pepper and use to dress the salad.

Heat 1-2cm sunflower oil in a large
frypan over medium heat. Fry the schnitzels
for 3-4 minutes each side until golden and
cooked through.

Slice the schnitzel thickly, then arrange on
the salad and serve sprinkled with chives.

Moroccan chicken with olives

Serves 4

8 free-range chicken pieces
1/4 cup (60ml) olive oil
3 garlic cloves, finely chopped
1 tbs grated ginger
2 lemons, cut into wedges
3 tbs Moroccan spice mix*
300ml hot chicken stock
1 cup (120g) pitted green olives
Couscous, to serve

Preheat the oven to 180°C.

Place the chicken, oil, garlic, ginger, lemon and spice mix in a roasting pan. Season with pepper and a little salt. Using your hands, rub the spice mixture into the chicken to coat well. Roast, turning occasionally, for 45 minutes. Add the stock and olives and return to the oven, basting occasionally, for a further 15 minutes until the chicken is cooked.

Transfer the chicken to a serving dish, cover loosely with foil and set aside. Skim any excess oil from the roasting pan, then place the pan with remaining juices and olives on the stove over medium heat. Simmer, stirring occasionally, for 5-7 minutes until thickened and reduced. Pour over the chicken, then serve with couscous.

* Available from selected supermarkets, delis and gourmet shops (see Glossary).

Chicken involtini with smoked mozzarella

Serves 4

Smoked mozzarella (scamorza) gives a wonderful flavour to this
dish, but if you can't find it at the deli, use bocconcini instead.

4 x 150g free-range chicken breast fillets
1/4 cup (60ml) olive oil
2 tbs chopped oregano leaves
2 tbs chopped flat-leaf parsley
1 garlic clove, chopped
16-24 pancetta slices (from a
    flat piece)*
250g smoked mozzarella (scamorza)*
    or bocconcini, thinly sliced
200g jar roasted red and yellow capsicum
    strips (see Glossary), drained
Soft polenta (see Basics, p 246),
    to serve (optional)

Lay the chicken fillets on a board between
pieces of plastic wrap. Beat with a rolling pin
to flatten to an even thickness of about 2cm.

Combine 1 tablespoon of oil with the
oregano, parsley and garlic in a bowl. Season.

Lay 4-6 pancetta slices, overlapping, on the
workbench (so they form a sheet large enough
to enclose the chicken). Place a chicken fillet
across the slices, brush with a little of the oil
mixture, then top with a layer of mozzarella
slices and capsicum pieces. Starting at one
short end, roll up the chicken and filling,
using the pancetta to completely enclose.
Tie in 2-3 places with kitchen string. Repeat
with remaining chicken fillets and filling.

Chill the involtini for 15 minutes while
you preheat the oven to 180°C.

Heat the remaining oil in a large ovenproof
frypan over medium-high heat. Cook the
chicken, turning, for 2-3 minutes until browned
all over. Transfer to the oven for 10 minutes
until chicken is cooked and cheese is melted.

Remove the rolls from the oven and slice
thickly. Serve with polenta, if desired.

* Available from delis and gourmet shops.

Quail with hummus and pomegranate

Serves 6

2 tbs ras el hanout*
¹/₄ cup (60ml) olive oil
6 quails*, butterflied
1 red onion, thinly sliced
1 tbs pine nuts
1 tsp cumin seeds
1 tsp ground cinnamon
1 tsp ground coriander
Seeds of 1 pomegranate*
2 tbs chopped flat-leaf parsley
Hummus, to serve

Combine ras el hanout and 2 tablespoons oil in a bowl. Add the quail and toss to coat in the mixture. Set aside for 15 minutes to marinate.

Meanwhile, heat remaining 1 tablespoon oil in a large non-stick frypan over medium-low heat. Add the onion and ¹/₂ teaspoon salt and cook, stirring, for 2-3 minutes until softened. Add nuts, and spices and cook, stirring, for a further 3 minutes until the nuts start to brown. Remove from the pan and set aside.

Preheat a barbecue hotplate or the cleaned frypan over high heat. Cook the quail (in batches if necessary) for 2-3 minutes each side until browned and cooked through. Cover loosely with foil and leave to rest for 5 minutes.

Arrange the quail on a platter, sprinkle with the onion mixture and pomegranate seeds, then garnish with parsley and serve with hummus.

* Ras el hanout is a Moroccan spice blend available from Middle Eastern and gourmet food shops (see Glossary); substitute Moroccan spice from supermarkets. Pomegranates are available from selected greengrocers in season. Butterflied quails are available from selected supermarkets, butchers and poultry shops.

Poached Asian-style turkey breast

Serves 6-8

Poaching turkey in Asian broth is a really simple way to cook it. Wonderful served hot or cold, this is a great alternative to traditional festive turkey dishes.

1 onion, quartered
1/2 cup (125ml) soy sauce
1/2 cup (125ml) Chinese rice wine
    (shaohsing)* or dry sherry
4 garlic cloves, bruised
2 tbs ginger matchsticks
4 strips pared orange rind
1 cinnamon quill
1 star anise
1 long red chilli, halved
1.2-1.5kg boned, rolled turkey breast
1 cup (120g) frozen peas
100g sugar snap peas, blanched
4 cups (200g) baby Asian salad leaves*
    or mizuna*
2 cups bean sprouts, trimmed
1 cup Thai basil leaves*
2 tbs rice vinegar
2 tsp sesame oil

Place the onion, soy sauce, wine, garlic, ginger, orange rind, cinnamon, star anise and chilli in a large saucepan. Add the turkey breast and enough cold water to cover. Bring to the boil, then decrease heat to low and simmer for 15 minutes. Remove from the heat, cover and set aside for 30 minutes to finish cooking. Remove turkey to a plate. Reserve 1/3 cup (80ml) of the poaching liquid and cool, discarding remaining liquid, onion and spices.

   Meanwhile, for the salad, blanch the frozen and sugar snap peas in a pan of boiling water for 1-2 minutes, then drain and rinse in cold water. Place in a bowl with the salad leaves, sprouts and basil. Whisk cooled poaching liquid with rice vinegar and sesame oil. Toss the salad with 2-3 tablespoons of the dressing.

   Slice the turkey, drizzle with the remaining dressing and serve with the salad.

* Chinese rice wine is available from Asian food shops; substitute dry sherry. Baby Asian salad leaves and Thai basil are available from selected supermarkets and greengrocers.

Maple-glazed duck

Serves 4

Duck marylands are a delicious alternative to chicken, and they're more affordable than you might think. This sticky barbecue sauce makes the perfect accompaniment.

4 duck marylands*
2 tbs pure maple syrup
1/3 cup (80ml) red wine
1/3 cup (80ml) soy sauce
1/3 cup (80ml) tomato sauce (ketchup)
1 tsp ground ginger
1 tbs mustard powder
2 garlic cloves, finely chopped
2 tbs sweet chilli sauce
Duck-fat fried potatoes (see Basics, p 246) and steamed green beans, to serve
Chopped flat-leaf parsley, to garnish

Preheat the oven to 180°C.

Place duck marylands, skin-side down, in a non-stick frypan over medium heat and cook for 3-4 minutes, allowing the fat to render from the duck. Once the skin is golden, turn and cook for a further 2-3 minutes. Transfer duck to a roasting pan (reserving the fat from the frypan to cook duck-fat fried potatoes).

Place the maple syrup, wine, soy, tomato sauce, ground ginger, mustard, garlic and sweet chilli in a bowl. Whisk until well combined and mustard powder has dissolved. Pour over the duck and cook in the oven, basting occasionally, for 30 minutes until the duck is cooked through and the skin is dark and sticky. Watch carefully – add a little water to the pan if the glaze is starting to burn. Remove from the oven, cover loosely with foil and set aside for 5 minutes to rest. Skim any excess fat from the sauce.

Serve the duck with potatoes and beans, drizzled with sauce and garnished with parsley.

* Order duck marylands from poultry shops and butchers.

Duck & shiitake mushroom pithiviers

Makes 8

To accompany the pies, ask for some plum sauce and spring onion sauce at the Asian barbecue shop when you buy your duck. Small versions of these make great cocktail food.

50g dried shiitake mushrooms*, soaked
  in boiling water for 15 minutes
1 tbs olive oil
1 onion, finely chopped
1 tbs grated ginger
2 garlic cloves, crushed
2 tsp plain flour
1 tsp five-spice powder
1 tbs soy sauce
1 Chinese barbecued duck*,
  meat cut into small pieces,
  skin and bones discarded
4 sheets frozen puff pastry, thawed
1 egg, beaten
Spring onion & ginger sauce
  and plum sauce, to serve

Drain the mushrooms, reserving ½ cup (125ml) of the soaking liquid, then chop.

Heat the oil in a frypan over medium heat. Add the onion and cook, stirring, for 2-3 minutes until soft. Add the ginger, garlic and mushrooms and cook, stirring, for 1-2 minutes. Add the flour and five-spice, stir to combine, then add the reserved soaking liquid and cook, stirring, for 2 minutes or until the sauce thickens. Stir in the soy and duck, then season with salt to taste. Remove from the heat and allow to cool.

Preheat the oven to 180°C. Using a 12cm cutter, cut 4 rounds from each pastry sheet. Place 8 rounds on a large lined baking tray. Divide filling among the pastry rounds, leaving a 1.5cm border. Brush edges with a little egg, then top with remaining pastry and press to seal. Use a small sharp knife to lightly score a 1cm border around the edge of each pithivier and a spiral pattern over the top. Brush with more beaten egg, then bake for 25 minutes or until puffed and golden. Serve with the spring onion and plum sauces.

* Dried shiitakes are available from Asian food shops. Chinese barbecued duck is available from Asian barbecue shops.

Confit duck with lentil & orange salad

Serves 4

Confit duck legs are quite readily available these days and so quick and easy to cook, as the slow-cooking process they've been through guarantees they'll be tender.

4 confit duck legs*
2 oranges
3 tsp red wine vinegar
1 tsp wholegrain mustard
¼ cup (60ml) walnut oil*
   or extra virgin olive oil
400g can brown lentils, rinsed
1 bunch watercress, sprigs picked
½ red onion, thinly sliced

Preheat the oven to 180°C. Line a baking tray with baking paper.

Scrape excess fat from the duck, then place the duck on the tray and roast for 15 minutes until browned and heated through.

Meanwhile, remove the peel and pith from the oranges, then use a sharp knife to segment the flesh over a bowl to catch any juice. Set the segments aside in a large bowl, then add the vinegar, mustard and oil to the juice. Season with salt and pepper and whisk to combine.

Add the lentils, watercress sprigs and sliced red onion to the orange segments, then toss with half the dressing.

Divide the salad among 4 serving plates, top with the confit duck and drizzle over the remaining dressing.

* Duck confit is available from gourmet food shops and selected poultry shops and butchers. Walnut oil is available from gourmet food shops and delis.

Sukiyaki beef with edamame and sushi rice

Serves 4

In summer, I like to chargrill the steaks on the barbecue and simply make the sauce in a pan.

200g podded frozen edamame
  (soybeans)*
1 tbs olive oil
4 x 180g beef eye fillet steaks
3cm piece ginger, thinly sliced
3 small red chillies, seeds removed,
  thinly sliced
2 tbs dark soy sauce
2 tbs sake
2 tbs mirin (sweet Japanese rice wine)*
Shredded spring onion, to garnish
Wasabi paste*, to serve

Sushi rice
1$^{1}/_{2}$ cups (300g) sushi rice
2$^{1}/_{2}$ tbs caster sugar
$^{1}/_{4}$ cup (60ml) rice vinegar

For the sushi rice, wash rice under cold water until water runs clear. Place in a pan with 450ml water, cover and slowly bring to the boil. Boil for 3 minutes, then reduce heat to low and cook for 9 minutes. Remove from the heat and stand, covered, for 10 minutes until rice is tender.

Meanwhile, place sugar and vinegar in a pan with 1 tablespoon salt and bring to the boil. Cool slightly, then stir into the rice.

Cook edamame in boiling salted water for 5 minutes until tender, then drain. Keep warm.

Heat oil in a large frypan over medium-high heat. Season steaks, then cook, turning to seal on all sides, for 5 minutes. Cover loosely with foil and set aside while you make the sauce.

Return frypan to medium-high heat, add ginger and chilli and cook for 1-2 minutes until softened. Add soy sauce, sake and mirin and cook, stirring, until thick and sticky. Cut each steak into cubes, then reassemble on the rice. Pour over sauce, scatter with edamame and spring onion, then serve with wasabi.

* Available from Asian food shops and selected supermarkets.

Braciola

Serves 6-8

Braciole are often small rolls of sliced beef braised in tomato sauce. This version uses a whole beef fillet and makes a wonderful main course when entertaining.

2 garlic cloves
4 spring onions, chopped
1/4 cup chopped flat-leaf parsley
5 slices mild salami (such as sopressa or Hungarian salami), roughly chopped
250g fontina* or Taleggio* cheese, chopped
1/2 cup (40g) grated parmesan
1/2 cup (35g) fresh breadcrumbs, toasted
1/3 cup (50g) sundried tomatoes, drained
1.5kg piece centre-cut beef eye fillet
1/3 cup (80ml) olive oil
350g vine-ripened cherry tomatoes, separated into sprigs

Place the garlic, spring onion, parsley, salami, fontina, parmesan, breadcrumbs and sundried tomatoes in a food processor, season with salt and pepper and pulse a few times to combine.

Cut 6 long pieces of kitchen string. Use a sharp knife to butterfly the beef fillet, slicing the fillet almost all the way through. Open the meat out like a book and pound with a rolling pin to flatten slightly. Spread the stuffing over the beef, leaving a 3cm border, then roll up from the side nearest to you. Tie with the string to secure, then enclose tightly in plastic wrap and chill for at least 1 hour, preferably overnight.

Preheat the oven to 200°C.

Heat the oil in a large frypan or flameproof roasting pan over high heat. Brown the beef on all sides, then place in the oven and roast for 25 minutes, adding the cherry tomatoes for the final 5 minutes, until the beef is medium-rare and the tomatoes have wilted slightly. Remove from the oven, cover loosely with foil and set aside to rest for 10 minutes.

Remove the string from the beef, then cut into thick slices and serve with the tomatoes.

* Available from delis and gourmet food shops.

Rib-eye with espresso & mushroom sauce

Serves 4

I know it sounds like a strange combination but trust me,
a shot of espresso lifts this sauce to another level.

20g dried porcini mushrooms*
1/3 cup (80ml) hot espresso coffee
4 x 250g beef rib-eye steaks
   on the bone
1/3 cup (80ml) olive oil
30g unsalted butter, chilled, chopped
1 garlic clove, finely chopped
2 tbs chopped thyme leaves,
   plus sprigs to garnish
250g Swiss brown mushrooms, sliced
1/3 cup (80ml) red wine
100ml veal* or beef stock
1/3 cup (80ml) dry Marsala*
Mashed potato, to serve

Place the porcini in a bowl, pour over the hot espresso and set aside for 15 minutes. Strain, reserving the liquid, and chop any large porcini.

Season the steaks with salt and pepper. Heat the oil in a frypan over medium-high heat. Add the steaks and cook for 2-3 minutes each side for medium-rare, or until cooked to your liking. Transfer to a plate, cover loosely with foil and set aside while you make the sauce.

Drain any excess fat from the frypan, add half the butter and place over medium heat. When the butter is melted, add the garlic, porcini, thyme and Swiss brown mushrooms and cook, stirring, for 2 minutes. Add the red wine, reserved soaking liquid, stock and Marsala and simmer until the sauce is reduced by half. Add the remaining butter, season with salt and pepper and stir to combine.

Serve the steaks on mash with the espresso and mushroom sauce poured over, garnished with thyme sprigs, if desired.

* Dried porcinis and veal stock are available from gourmet food shops and greengrocers. Dry Marsala is available from bottle shops.

Eye fillet with raspberry sauce

Serves 4

In Scandinavia, it's quite common to serve tart berry sauces with game and red meat. Try blueberries or redcurrants in season and adjust the sugar to taste.

1 tbs olive oil
10g unsalted butter
4 x 180g beef eye fillet steaks
1 cup (250ml) red wine
2 tbs caster sugar
250g raspberries
1 cup (250ml) good-quality beef stock
3 tbs creme fraiche or sour cream
Potato mash and steamed green beans,
   to serve

Place the oil and butter in a frypan over high heat. Season the steaks with salt and pepper and cook for 2-3 minutes each side until browned and cooked to medium-rare (or until done to your liking). Transfer to a plate, cover loosely with foil and set aside while you make the sauce.

Return the pan to medium heat and add the red wine, sugar and most of the raspberries (reserving about $1/2$ cup to garnish). Cook, stirring, for 2-3 minutes until the fruit has broken down. Add the stock and cook for 3-4 minutes until syrupy. Whisk in the creme fraiche or sour cream and season to taste. Strain the sauce, discarding the solids, and return to the pan. Add any beef resting juices and the reserved berries to the pan and stir until heated through.

Serve the steaks on potato mash and green beans, drizzled with the raspberry sauce.

Beef carpaccio with preserved lemon salad

Serves 4-6

600g piece beef eye fillet
1 cup (300g) whole egg mayonnaise
1 tbs Worcestershire sauce
2 tbs milk
1 tbs lemon juice
2 tbs extra virgin olive oil
1 tbs baby capers, rinsed
1/2 bunch flat-leaf parsley,
    leaves picked
1/4 preserved lemon*, white pith and
    flesh removed, skin thinly sliced

Chill the beef in the freezer for 30 minutes so it will be easier to slice.

Meanwhile, whisk mayonnaise, Worcestershire sauce, milk and half the lemon juice together in a small bowl and season with salt and pepper.

Whisk oil and remaining lemon juice in a bowl, season, then add capers, parsley and preserved lemon and toss to combine.

Use a sharp knife to slice the beef fillet as thinly as possible. Place slices between sheets of baking paper, then gently roll with a rolling pin to make them thinner, without tearing.

Arrange the beef slices on a platter or individual plates. Scatter over the salad, then drizzle with the dressing and serve.

* Available from gourmet food shops and delis.

Posh pie and peas

Makes 6

2 tbs olive oil, plus extra if needed
1 onion, finely chopped
1 celery stalk, finely chopped
1 small carrot, finely chopped
600g lean diced lamb
2 tbs plain flour, seasoned with
    salt and pepper
1 tbs tomato paste
1 cup (250ml) lager
1½ cups (375ml) beef stock
2 tsp Vegemite
1 tbs Worcestershire sauce
2 tbs chopped mint leaves,
    plus sprigs to garnish
8 sheets frozen butter puff
    pastry, thawed
1 egg, lightly beaten
2 cups (240g) frozen peas

Place 1 tablespoon of the oil in a deep frypan or casserole over medium-high heat. Add the onion, celery and carrot and cook, stirring, for 2-3 minutes until softened. Transfer to a bowl.

Return the pan to the heat with the remaining oil. Toss lamb in the seasoned flour. In 2 batches, cook the lamb for 3-4 minutes to brown, adding more oil if needed. Return all the lamb to the pan with onion mixture and tomato paste. Cook, stirring, for 1 minute, then add lager, stock, Vegemite and Worcestershire sauce. Season, bring to the boil, then simmer over low heat for 1 hour or until the lamb is very tender. Strain the meat mixture, reserving the gravy in a saucepan. Stir mint into the meat mixture, then cool.

Preheat the oven to 190°C. Cut six 14cm and six 9cm rounds from the pastry. Use the larger rounds to line 6 greased 1 cup (250ml) dariole moulds or 12cm pie pans. Divide the cooled filling among the pies. Brush edges of smaller pastry rounds with a little beaten egg, then use to top the pies, pressing the edges to seal. Trim any excess, then brush the top of each pie with more egg. Cut small holes in the top for steam to escape, then bake for 35 minutes until golden (cover loosely with foil if browning too quickly).

Meanwhile, cook peas in boiling salted water for 2-3 minutes, then drain. Warm reserved gravy. Run a knife around the edge of each pie dish, then transfer pies to plates. Serve topped with peas, gravy and mint.

Lamb with red curry sauce and Thai basil

Serves 4

400ml coconut milk
2-3 tbs Thai red curry paste (to taste)
3/4 cup (75g) roasted peanuts, ground,
   plus extra chopped to garnish
2 tbs grated palm sugar*
5 kaffir lime leaves*, finely shredded
1/4 cup (60ml) Thai fish sauce
2 x 200g lamb backstraps
1 1/2 tbs sunflower oil
4 Asian red eschalots*, thinly sliced
1 green chilli, sliced
150g bean sprouts, trimmed
Steamed jasmine rice, to serve
Juice of 1 lime
1 bunch Thai basil*, leaves picked
Coriander sprigs, to garnish

Place 200ml of the coconut milk and the curry paste in a wok over medium-high heat and bring to the boil. Add the remaining 200ml coconut milk and simmer for 5 minutes. Add the ground peanuts, sugar, kaffir lime leaves and fish sauce and simmer for 2 minutes, then keep warm over low heat while you cook the lamb.

Season the lamb with salt and pepper. Heat 1/2 tablespoon oil in a frypan over high heat. Add the lamb and cook, turning to brown on all sides, for 5 minutes for medium-rare (or until done to your liking). Transfer to a plate and cover loosely with foil.

Return the cleaned pan to low heat, then add the remaining oil. Add the eschalot and chilli and cook for 1 minute until softened. Add the bean sprouts and stir for 30 seconds.

Slice the lamb and divide among serving plates with steamed rice. Stir the lime juice into the curry sauce, then spoon over the lamb with the sprout mixture and basil. Garnish with coriander and extra chopped peanuts.
* Available from Asian food shops and selected greengrocers.

Lamb cutlets with Moroccan beans

Serves 4

3 tbs chermoula paste*
2 tbs olive oil
12 lamb cutlets
1 onion, finely chopped
2 x 400g cans borlotti beans,
    drained, rinsed
3 tbs honey
1/2 cup (125ml) vegetable stock
2 tbs chopped coriander leaves
Thick Greek-style yoghurt, to serve

Combine 1 tablespoon of the chermoula with 1 tablespoon of the oil. Toss the lamb in the mixture to coat and set aside.

Place the remaining oil in a frypan over medium heat. Add the onion and cook, stirring, for 2-3 minutes until beginning to soften. Add the remaining 2 tablespoons of chermoula and stir briefly until fragrant, then add the beans, honey and stock. Simmer for 5 minutes until slightly thickened. Keep warm.

Preheat a barbecue or chargrill pan to high. Cook the lamb cutlets for 1-2 minutes each side until browned but still pink in the centre.

Divide the beans among 4 serving plates, then top with the lamb cutlets and serve with coriander and yoghurt .

* Chermoula (a North African herb and spice paste) is available from delis and gourmet shops (see Glossary).

Shortcut roast lamb with caramelised onion couscous

Serves 4-6

For a midweek roast, choose an easy-carve cut of meat that requires less cooking time.

3 tsp each of ground cumin,
   ground coriander and paprika
3 garlic cloves, crushed
$^1/_3$ cup (80ml) olive oil
1.5kg easy-carve lamb leg
2 onions, sliced
2 tbs chopped thyme leaves
$1^1/_2$ tbs caster sugar
100ml balsamic vinegar
1 cup (200g) couscous
20g unsalted butter
1 cup (100g) toasted walnuts, chopped
2 tbs chopped flat-leaf parsley
2 tbs walnut oil* or extra virgin olive oil

Preheat the oven to 180°C.

Stir the spices with garlic and 2 tablespoons of the olive oil. Spread the spice paste all over the lamb, then place in a roasting pan and roast for 1 hour.

Meanwhile, heat the remaining olive oil in a frypan over medium-low heat. Add the onion, thyme, 1 teaspoon sea salt and plenty of black pepper. Cook for 4-6 minutes until the onion starts to caramelise. Stir in the sugar and vinegar, decrease the heat to low and cook, stirring occasionally, for 4-5 minutes until almost all the liquid has been absorbed.

Remove lamb from the oven, cover loosely with foil and set aside to rest in a warm place while you make the couscous.

Place the couscous in a bowl and pour over 400ml boiling water. Cover with plastic wrap and stand for 5 minutes. Fluff the couscous grains with a fork, then stir in the caramelised onion, butter, walnuts, parsley and oil. Serve with the roast lamb.

* Available from gourmet food shops.

Olive-crusted lamb racks with chickpea salad

Serves 4

20 pitted kalamata olives
$^1/_4$ cup rosemary leaves
$^1/_3$ cup (80ml) olive oil
2 x 4-cutlet lamb racks, french-trimmed
400g can chickpeas, drained, rinsed
250g punnet cherry tomatoes,
    quartered
1 Lebanese cucumber, peeled,
    seeds removed, chopped
1 cup mint leaves
1 cup basil leaves
Juice of 1 lemon
150g Persian (marinated) feta*,
    drained, crumbled

Preheat the oven to 200°C.

Mix the olives, rosemary and 2 tablespoons of the oil in a food processor to form a thick paste.

Heat 1 tablespoon of the oil in a frypan over medium-high heat. Season the lamb with salt and pepper and cook racks, one at a time, for 3-4 minutes until browned all over. Cool slightly, then press the paste onto the meaty side of the lamb. Place in a roasting pan and roast for 20 minutes for medium-rare (or until done to your liking), then cover loosely with foil and set aside to rest while you make the salad.

Place the chickpeas, tomato, cucumber, mint and basil in a bowl. In a separate bowl, combine the remaining 1 tablespoon of oil with the lemon juice, season with salt and pepper and use to dress the salad. Scatter the salad with the cheese. Halve each lamb rack, then serve with the salad.

* Persian feta is available from delis and selected supermarkets.

XO pork stir-fry with Asian greens

Serves 4

XO is a spicy, seafood-based sauce that was once only used by Cantonese restaurants, but is now readily available in Asian food shops and delis to give an authentic flavour.

3 tbs XO sauce*
1/2 tsp sesame oil
1 1/2 tsp chilli jam
1 tbs honey
1 tbs light soy sauce
1 tbs sunflower oil
300g pork fillet, thinly sliced
1 garlic clove, thinly sliced
3cm piece ginger, thinly sliced
3 spring onions, thinly sliced
1 tbs Chinese rice wine (shaohsing)*
1 bunch Chinese broccoli (gai lan)
  or other Asian greens
Steamed rice, to serve

Combine the XO sauce, sesame oil, chilli jam, honey and soy sauce in a bowl.

Heat the sunflower oil in a wok over high heat. When the oil is smoking, add half the pork and stir-fry for 1-2 minutes until browned. Remove and repeat with the remaining pork.

Decrease the heat to medium and return all the browned pork to the wok. Add the garlic, ginger and half the onion and stir-fry for 1 minute until fragrant. Add the wine and XO mixture and stir-fry for a further minute.

Meanwhile, steam the Chinese broccoli over a pan of boiling water for 2-3 minutes until just tender and bright green. Serve with the pork stir-fry on steamed rice.

* Available from Asian food shops.

Fennel-roasted pork with apple sauce

Serves 4

Pork racks are a great solution for a mid-week roast, as they don't take long to cook and you still get delicious crackling!

2 tsp fennel seeds
1/2 tsp dried chilli flakes
2 tbs fresh rosemary leaves
1 tbs olive oil
1kg pork rack (4 cutlets), skin scored

Apple sauce
11/3 cups (300g) caster sugar
100ml apple cider vinegar
1/2 vanilla bean, split, seeds scraped
1 cinnamon quill
5 Granny Smith apples, peeled, cored, chopped
Juice of 1/2 lemon

Preheat the oven to 220°C and line a baking tray with baking paper.

Grind the fennel seeds, chilli, rosemary and 2 teaspoons sea salt in a mortar and pestle until crushed. Combine with the olive oil and rub into the pork well. Place on the tray and roast for 25 minutes, then decrease the oven temperature to 180°C and roast for a further 10 minutes until the crackling is crisp and meat is just cooked through.

Meanwhile, for the sauce, place the sugar, vinegar, vanilla pod and seeds, and cinnamon in a saucepan over medium heat and stir until the sugar dissolves. Simmer for 5 minutes, then add the apple and lemon juice and cook, stirring occasionally, for 15-20 minutes until the apple is soft. Cool slightly, then discard the vanilla and cinnamon. Place in a blender and puree until smooth. The sauce will keep in an airtight container in the fridge for 1 week.

Remove the pork from the oven, cover loosely with foil and leave to rest for 10-15 minutes. Slice the pork into cutlets and serve with the apple sauce.

Charcuterie plate with grilled onion salad

Serves 4

Sometimes a grazing supper is just the thing. Pick up some good-quality smallgoods from a deli, and if you don't have time to make the onion salad, ready-made onion marmalade will do.

2 onions, cut into 1cm-thick rounds
Olive oil, to brush
1/4 cup (60ml) red wine vinegar
1/4 firmly packed cup (50g) brown sugar
200g sliced cured meats (such as ham, prosciutto and salami)
100g piece pork terrine or paté
Cornichons (small pickled cucumbers), pickled onions, wholegrain mustard and toasted or grilled bread, to serve

Brush the onion with oil. Place a chargrill pan over high heat and when it's very hot, cook the onion rounds on both sides until charred and softened.

Meanwhile, combine the vinegar and sugar in a bowl, stirring to dissolve the sugar. Add the hot onions, season with salt and pepper and toss gently. Leave to cool.

Arrange the sliced meats and terrine or paté on a platter. Serve with the onion salad, cornichons, pickled onions, mustard and bread.

Pork with Caribbean pineapple sauce

Serves 4

4 x 280g pork loin chops
1 tbs olive oil
$^1/_2$ ripe pineapple, peeled,
    cut into 1cm cubes
2 eschalots, finely chopped
2 long red chillies, seeds removed,
    finely chopped
$^1/_3$ cup (75g) caster sugar
100ml dark rum
1 tbs red wine vinegar
Steamed snow peas, to serve

Preheat the oven to 170°C.

Season the chops with salt and pepper. Heat the oil in a large frypan over medium-high heat. Add the chops and brown for 2-3 minutes each side, then transfer to a baking tray. Place in the oven and bake for 10 minutes until cooked through.

Meanwhile, return the pan to the heat and add the pineapple, eschalot and chilli. Cook, stirring, for 2-3 minutes until the eschalot has softened. Add the sugar, rum and vinegar and cook, stirring, for 3-4 minutes until the sauce is reduced and sticky.

Divide the pork chops among plates, top with the pineapple sauce and serve with snow peas.

Italian sausage rolls

Makes 36

I love a good sausage roll, and it's handy to keep some uncooked in the freezer, ready to pop in the oven when friends call in or hungry teenagers need a snack. They're a must at a Christmas drinks party, too.

500g good-quality Italian pork sausages
1 zucchini, coarsely grated,
    squeezed of excess liquid
1¼ cups (100g) grated parmesan
1 onion, grated
2 tbs sundried tomato pesto
2 eggs
3 sheets frozen puff pastry, thawed
Tomato chutney, to serve

Preheat the oven to 180°C and line a large baking tray with baking paper.

Squeeze the sausages from their casings (discarding casings), and place meat in a bowl with the zucchini, parmesan, onion, sundried tomato pesto and 1 lightly beaten egg. Using damp hands, combine the mixture well.

Cut each pastry sheet in half to make 6 rectangles. Lightly beat the remaining egg.

Divide the filling into 6 portions, then roll into sausage shapes the length of the pastry.

Place 1 filling portion down one side of a pastry rectangle and lightly brush the opposite side with a little egg. Roll up to enclose the filling, pressing to seal where the pastry overlaps. Turn seam-side down and cut on an angle into 6 small sausage rolls, then place on the tray. Repeat with the remaining filling and pastry, then brush the tops with the remaining beaten egg and bake for 20-25 minutes until puffed and golden. Serve with tomato chutney.

Homestyle meatloaf

Serves 4-6

Sweet canned cherry tomatoes from the deli make a quick sauce for this meatloaf.
Serve it with mash and you have a guaranteed family favourite.

3 cups (210g) fresh breadcrumbs
1/2 cup (125ml) milk
500g lean beef mince
500g lean pork mince
1 onion, grated
1 tsp finely grated lemon zest
3 garlic cloves, crushed
1 roasted capsicum (or use 170g
   ready-roasted capsicum slices),
   chopped
2 tbs chopped oregano leaves,
   plus whole leaves to garnish
1/4 cup finely chopped flat-leaf parsley
2 tbs tomato sauce (ketchup)
1 tbs Worcestershire sauce
2 eggs, plus 1 extra yolk
400g can cherry tomatoes*

Preheat the oven to 170°C and lightly grease
a 22cm x 14cm loaf pan or terrine. Soak the
crumbs in the milk for 10 minutes.

Place the soaked crumbs in a large bowl
with the remaining ingredients (except the
tomatoes). Season with salt and pepper,
then mix well with your hands to combine.
Pack the mixture into the loaf pan and smooth
the top. Cover with a piece of baking paper,
then foil. Place on a baking tray and bake for
45 minutes, then cook uncovered for a further
15 minutes to brown the top.

Remove from the oven, then carefully drain
any liquid from the pan into a saucepan. Cover
the meatloaf loosely with foil to keep warm.

Add the cherry tomatoes to the saucepan,
season with salt and pepper and bring to
the boil. Simmer over medium-low heat
for 10 minutes until sauce has thickened.

Place the meatloaf on a serving platter,
pour over the tomato sauce and serve
garnished with oregano leaves.

* Available from delis.

Moroccan cottage pie

Serves 4-6

Cottage pie is a great midweek dinner, and here Moroccan spices take it to another level. If you want a golden crust, pop the potato-covered dish under the grill for 3-4 minutes.

2 tbs olive oil
1 onion, finely chopped
2 garlic cloves, chopped
650g lamb mince
1 tsp ground cumin
1 tsp ground cinnamon
1/2 tsp ground ginger
1/2 tsp chilli powder
2 tsp ground turmeric
2 tbs tomato paste
150ml red wine
150ml beef stock
1/2 cup (80g) roughly chopped
    pitted green olives
1/3 cup chopped mint leaves,
    plus small leaves to garnish
1kg pontiac potatoes, peeled,
    chopped
40g unsalted butter, chopped
1/2 cup (120g) creme fraiche
    or sour cream

Heat the oil in a large saucepan over medium-low heat. Add the onion and garlic and cook, stirring, for 2-3 minutes until softened. Add the mince and cook, stirring, for 5-6 minutes until the meat is browned.

Add the dry spices (reserving 1 teaspoon turmeric for the potato) and the tomato paste, then cook for a further minute. Add the wine and stock, bring to a simmer, then decrease heat to low and cook for 15-18 minutes until the meat is cooked and the sauce has thickened. Stir in the olives and mint. Transfer the mixture to a serving dish and set aside.

Meanwhile, cook the potato and remaining turmeric in a saucepan of boiling salted water for 10-12 minutes until tender. Drain well and pass through a potato ricer or mash well. Season with salt and pepper. Stir in the butter and creme fraiche or sour cream.

Spread the mashed potato over the mince, then serve garnished with mint leaves.

Pork patties with mango salsa

Makes 8

1 large red onion, chopped
1 tsp ground cumin
1 tsp ground coriander
500g lean pork mince
3/4 cup (50g) fresh breadcrumbs
1 small red chilli, seeds removed,
  finely chopped
2 tsp korma curry paste
3cm piece fresh ginger, grated
2 garlic cloves
2 tbs chopped flat-leaf parsley
2 tbs sunflower oil
Baby spinach leaves, to garnish
  (optional)

Mango salsa

1 tbs sunflower oil
1/2 tsp black mustard seeds
12 fresh curry leaves*
1 tbs brown sugar
1 small red chilli, seeds removed,
  finely chopped
1 large mango, peeled, flesh chopped
2 tsp fresh lime juice

Place all the ingredients except the oil and spinach in a food processor, season, then pulse to combine. With damp hands, form the mixture into 8 patties, then chill for 10 minutes to firm up.

Meanwhile, for the salsa, heat the oil in a frypan over medium-low heat. Add the mustard seeds and curry leaves and cook, stirring, for 1 minute until fragrant and the leaves are crisp. Transfer to a bowl and mix gently with the remaining ingredients. Season with salt and pepper, then set aside.

Heat the 2 tablespoons of oil in a frypan over medium-high heat. Add the patties and cook for 3-4 minutes on each side until cooked through. Serve with mango salsa and garnish with spinach if desired.

* Fresh curry leaves are available from selected greengrocers and Asian food shops.

Swedish meatballs

Makes 24

Forget ready-made TV dinners, serve trays of this stylish supper
to the family and wait for the applause!

400g pork mince
1 egg
1 onion, grated
1¼ cups (85g) fresh breadcrumbs
½ tsp ground allspice
¼ tsp ground cloves
Pinch of nutmeg
1 tbs olive oil
20g unsalted butter
150ml beef stock
2 tbs brown sugar
Lingonberry sauce* (see Glossary)
    or cranberry sauce, sour cream,
    dill & parsley potatoes, baby cos
    leaves and cucumber slices, to serve

Place the mince, egg, onion, breadcrumbs
and dry spices in a food processor, season
with salt and pepper and process to combine.
With damp hands, form the mixture into
24 walnut-sized balls. Place on a baking
tray, cover with plastic wrap and chill in
the fridge for 15 minutes to firm up.

Heat the oil and butter in a frypan over
medium heat. In batches, cook the meatballs,
turning, for 3-4 minutes until golden. Remove
from the pan and set aside.

Wipe the frypan clean, then add the stock
and sugar. Cook over medium-low heat,
stirring, for 3-5 minutes until syrupy.

Return all the meatballs to the pan and
warm through, coating the meatballs in the
glaze, for a further 1-2 minutes until warmed
through. Serve the meatballs with sauce,
sour cream, potatoes, lettuce and cucumber.
* Available from selected delis.

Cevapi

Makes 10

These skinless sausages from the Balkans are easy to make at home,
and delicious served with ajvar (capsicum relish) and sour cream.

500g lean beef mince
100g lean lamb mince
250g lean pork mince
3 garlic cloves, finely chopped
1 tbs bicarbonate of soda
2 tbs paprika
Olive oil, to rub and drizzle
Ajvar relish*, sour cream
　　and rocket leaves, to serve

Place the mince, garlic, bicarbonate of soda
and paprika in a food processor, season with
2 teaspoons sea salt and lots of black pepper,
then pulse to just combine.

Using damp hands, form the mixture into
10 sausage shapes, then chill in the fridge
for at least 10 minutes to firm up.

Heat a chargrill pan, frypan or barbecue
hotplate over medium-high heat. Rub the
cevapi with a little oil and cook, turning, for
3-5 minutes until browned and cooked through.
Serve with ajvar relish and sour cream.
Sprinkle with black pepper, scatter with rocket
leaves and drizzle with a little extra olive oil.
* Available from delis.

A pizza for summer

Serves 4 as a snack

This is ideal to serve with drinks on a warm evening. If you can't find edible flowers, just use fresh herbs. And use the best extra virgin olive oil you can afford – it's all about quality, not quantity!

1 small garlic clove, crushed
1 tbs extra virgin olive oil,
　plus extra to drizzle
24cm plain woodfired pizza base*
2 tsp grated lemon zest
1/2 cup (120g) low-fat ricotta
1 tbs finely grated parmesan
Edible flowers and baby herbs,
　to garnish
Squeeze of fresh lemon juice

Preheat the oven to 200°C.

Infuse the garlic in the oil for 10 minutes.

Brush the pizza base with the garlic oil and bake in the oven for 5-6 minutes until crisp and warmed through.

Combine the lemon zest and ricotta in a bowl and season with salt and pepper. Sprinkle the pizza base with the parmesan, then dot with the ricotta mixture and scatter with the flowers and herbs. Drizzle with a little extra oil and a squeeze of lemon, then cut into wedges and serve.

* Woodfired pizza bases are available from delis and selected supermarkets.

Crockpot-au-feu

Serves 4

Pot-au-feu is a classic French dish in which more mature chicken benefits from slow cooking. Throw all the ingredients in a slow-cooker (crockpot) in the morning for a no-fuss dinner that night. You can freeze any leftover stock, too.

1.6kg free-range chicken
1 large onion, chopped
1 bouquet garni*
1 cup (250ml) white wine
1 cup (250ml) chicken stock
4 baby leeks, trimmed
1 bunch baby (Dutch) carrots,
    ends trimmed
4 potatoes, peeled, chopped
100g thin green beans, ends trimmed
Chopped flat-leaf parsley, to sprinkle
Toasted baguette and low-fat ricotta,
    to serve

Season the chicken and truss with string. Place the chicken and onion in a slow cooker. Add the bouquet garni, wine, stock and enough water to cover. Season with salt and pepper and cover with the lid. Cook on a low heat for 6-8 hours until the chicken is tender and cooked. Add the leeks, carrots and potato and cook for a further hour, adding the green beans for the final 10 minutes of cooking.

Remove the chicken and slice. Divide the chicken, vegetables and some of the poaching liquid among serving bowls. Season well with salt and pepper and sprinkle with parsley. Serve with toasted baguette and ricotta.
* To make a bouquet garni, tie together a few bay leaves, parsley sprigs and thyme sprigs with kitchen string.

Steamed eggplant with tofu and snow peas

Serves 4

1 large eggplant, cut into 3cm chunks
100g snow peas, trimmed
$^1/_2$ cup (125ml) Chinese black
   (chinkiang) vinegar*
$^1/_3$ cup (80ml) Chinese rice wine
   (shaohsing)*
3 garlic cloves, finely chopped
2 tbs brown sugar
2 tbs light soy sauce
1 tsp sesame oil
1 tbs grated ginger
$^1/_3$ cup (80ml) vegetable stock or water
250g silken firm tofu,
   cut into 3cm cubes
2 tbs toasted sesame seeds
Steamed rice, to serve

Place the eggplant in a steamer over a pan of boiling water and steam for 10 minutes until tender, adding the snow peas for the last 2 minutes of cooking.

Meanwhile, place the vinegar, wine, garlic, sugar, soy sauce, oil, ginger and stock or water in a deep frypan over low heat. Cook, stirring, for 2 minutes or until the sugar has dissolved.

Add the steamed eggplant and snow peas to the frypan with the tofu, then toss gently to combine. Garnish with sesame seeds and serve with steamed rice.

* Available from Asian food shops.

Wonton soup

Serves 4

1.5L (6 cups) salt-reduced
  chicken stock
1 tbs ginger matchsticks
1 1/2 tbs light soy sauce
1 tsp caster sugar
1/2 tsp sesame oil, plus extra to serve
220g packet chicken or prawn wontons*
1 bunch baby bok choy,
  leaves separated
Thinly sliced spring onion and chilli, and
  mint and coriander leaves, to serve

Place the stock in a large saucepan and bring to the boil. Decrease the heat to medium and stir in the ginger, soy sauce, sugar and sesame oil.

Drop the wontons into the stock and simmer for 5 minutes or until cooked through. Remove from the heat, add the bok choy and stand until it wilts. Ladle the soup into serving bowls and garnish with spring onion, chilli and herbs, then drizzle with extra sesame oil.

* Available from Asian food shops.

Blueberry & apple jellies

Serves 4

You can choose any apple juice blend for this dish – apple and cranberry or blackcurrant work well. The Calvados is optional, but really adds punch to these jellies.

5 gold-strength gelatine leaves*
1 litre (4 cups) blueberry and
   apple juice
1/4 cup (60ml) Calvados*
4 tbs low-fat thick Greek-style yoghurt
Fresh blueberries, to serve
Dried apple slices (optional),
   to decorate

Soak the gelatine leaves in cold water for 5 minutes to soften.

Place the juice in a saucepan over medium heat and bring to a simmer. Squeeze the excess water from the gelatine leaves. Add the gelatine to the pan with the Calvados and stir well. Remove from the heat and set aside to cool. Pour the mixture into 4 glasses or bowls, cover with plastic wrap and place in the fridge until firm.

Serve the jellies topped with yoghurt and fresh blueberries.

* Gelatine leaves are available from gourmet food shops; always check the packet for setting instructions. Calvados is a dry apple brandy, available from selected bottle shops.

Classic chocolate pots

Makes 4

These little jars are the yoghurt pots you find in French supermarkets.
My husband, Phil, always despairs when I come home from France with
a suitcase full of them. They make great tealight candle holders, too.

½ cup (125ml) pure (thin) cream,
   plus whipped cream to serve
½ cup (125ml) milk
100g good-quality dark chocolate,
   chopped, plus extra shaved to sprinkle
3 egg yolks
2 tbs caster sugar
1 tsp vanilla extract

Preheat the oven to 160°C.

Place the cream and milk in a saucepan
over medium-low heat and bring to just below
boiling point. Add the chocolate and stir until
just melted, then remove from the heat.

Whisk the egg yolks, sugar and vanilla in
a bowl until just combined. Gradually whisk in
the chocolate mixture, combining well. Strain
into a jug, then pour into four 200ml heatproof
serving glasses or ramekins. Place in a
roasting pan and pour in enough hot water
to come halfway up the sides of the dishes.

Bake for 25 minutes or until just set with
a slight wobble. Remove from the water bath
and set aside to cool. Chill for at least 4 hours
or until ready to serve.

Serve the chocolate pots topped with
whipped cream and shaved chocolate.

Forrest Gump tart

Serves 6-8

I couldn't resist the name. Even if life is like a box of chocolates (you never know what you're going to get), it always seems a lot better after a slice of this tart!

250g frozen chocolate
   shortcrust pastry*, thawed
200ml thickened cream
300g good-quality dark chocolate,
   chopped
3 egg yolks
Cocoa powder, to dust
Assorted chocolates, to serve

Preheat the oven to 180°C. Grease a 35cm x 12cm rectangular loose-bottomed tart pan.

Roll out the pastry between 2 sheets of baking paper until slightly larger than the tart pan. Line the pan with the pastry, prick base with a fork, then chill for 15 minutes.

Line the pastry with baking paper and fill with pastry weights or uncooked rice. Blind-bake the tart shell for 15 minutes, then remove paper and weights and bake for a further 5 minutes until dry. Cool.

Meanwhile, place the cream in a saucepan over medium-low heat and bring to just below boiling point. Add the chocolate and stir until just melted, then remove from the heat and transfer to a bowl. Add the egg yolks and stir until smooth. Pour into the tart case, then chill in the fridge for 2-3 hours until set.

Transfer the tart to a serving platter, dust with cocoa, then gently press the chocolates into the filling. Slice and serve with coffee.
* Chocolate shortcrust pastry is available from delis and gourmet food shops (see Glossary), or use plain shortcrust pastry.

Mars bar trifle

Serves 4-6

I should rename this 'David's trifle', as our stylist David Morgan
polished most of it off it after the photoshoot.

6 gold-strength gelatine leaves*
250g caster sugar
30g cocoa powder
100ml Pedro Ximénez sherry*
   or Marsala*
12 sponge fingers (savoiardi)
   (about 120g), broken into pieces
4 x 60g Mars bars
350ml milk
300ml thickened cream, whipped

Soak 4 gelatine leaves in cold water for
5 minutes to soften. Meanwhile, place sugar
and 1 cup (250ml) water in a saucepan over
low heat, stirring to dissolve sugar. Increase
heat to medium and simmer for 4 minutes
until thickened slightly, then whisk in cocoa.

Squeeze the excess water from the gelatine
leaves and add the leaves to the syrup, stirring
to dissolve. Add the sherry and mix well. Strain
and set aside to cool slightly.

Place biscuits in a trifle bowl. Pour over cocoa
syrup, pressing the biscuits down well. Cover
and chill in the fridge for 2-3 hours to set.

For the second layer, soak the remaining
2 gelatine leaves in cold water for 5 minutes
until softened. Meanwhile, chop 3 Mars bars
and place in a pan with the milk over low heat,
stirring until melted and smooth. Squeeze
excess water from the gelatine, then add leaves
to the milk mixture and stir to dissolve. Cool
slightly, then pour over the chilled layer and
return to the fridge for 1-2 hours until set.

To serve, spread the whipped cream over the
trifle, then top with remaining sliced Mars bar.
* Gelatine leaves are available from gourmet
food shops – check packet for setting
instructions. Pedro Ximénez (a sweet, sticky
Spanish sherry) and Marsala are available
from selected bottle shops.

Molten mocha puddings

Makes 6

150g good-quality dark chocolate, finely chopped
125g unsalted butter, chopped
3 tsp instant espresso coffee
2 eggs, plus 2 extra yolks
1/2 cup (75g) pure icing sugar, sifted
1/4 cup (35g) plain flour, sifted
2 tsp cocoa powder, sifted
Fresh strawberries, halved, to serve

Preheat the oven to 200°C. Grease a 6-hole, 3/4 cup (185ml) capacity Texas muffin pan.

Place the chocolate, butter and coffee in a saucepan over low heat, stirring until melted and smooth. Remove from the heat and set aside to cool for 10 minutes.

Use electric beaters to beat the eggs, egg yolks and icing sugar together in a bowl until thick and pale. Gently fold in the flour and cooled chocolate mixture.

Spoon mixture into the muffin holes and bake for 10-12 minutes until the puddings look firm on the outside but are molten on the inside when pierced with a skewer. Set aside for 2-3 minutes to rest in the pan, then invert onto plates. Dust with cocoa powder and serve with strawberries.

Chocolate caramel slice

Makes 12

250g digestive or shortbread biscuits
70g unsalted butter, melted
1 cup (250ml) thickened cream
250g can caramel Top 'N' Fill
250g good-quality dark chocolate, chopped
4 egg yolks
1 tbs olive oil

Grease a 26cm x 18cm lamington pan and line with baking paper, leaving some overhanging the sides.

Crush the biscuits in a food processor, then add butter and pulse to combine well. Press into the base of the pan and chill for about 15 minutes until firm.

Place the cream and caramel in a saucepan and stir over low heat until combined and heated through. Remove from the heat, add 120g chocolate and stir until smooth.

Whisk the egg yolks in a bowl, then gradually whisk in the hot cream mixture. Pour the mixture over the biscuit base, then chill for about 2-3 hours until cooled and set.

Place the remaining chocolate and oil in a bowl set over a saucepan of simmering water (don't let the bowl touch the water) and stir until melted and smooth. Set aside to cool. Pour over the base and chill for 30 minutes or until set.

Use the overhanging baking paper to carefully lift the slice from the pan. Use a hot knife (dipped in hot water) to cut the slice into 12 bars. Keep in an airtight container in the fridge for up to 2 days.

Carrot cake

Serves 6-8

Everyone should have a simple carrot cake in their repertoire.
This one's always a winner at morning teas, fetes and barbecues.

1 cup (250ml) sunflower oil
1 cup (220g) caster sugar
3 eggs
$1^1/_2$ cups (225g) self-raising flour
1 large carrot, finely grated
Finely grated zest of 1 orange
$^3/_4$ cup (75g) toasted walnuts,
   finely chopped

Cream cheese frosting
50g unsalted butter
250g soft cream cheese
2 tbs pure icing sugar, sifted
1 tsp pure vanilla extract

Preheat the oven to 180°C. Grease an 18cm x 25cm lamington pan and line with baking paper, leaving some overhanging the sides.

Place the oil and sugar in a bowl and combine using a hand whisk. Whisk in the eggs, then sift in the flour and fold together to combine. Stir in the grated carrot, orange zest and $^1/_2$ cup (50g) of the walnuts.

Spread the mixture into the prepared pan and bake for 40 minutes or until a skewer inserted in the centre comes out clean. Cool in the pan for 10 minutes, then use the overhanging paper to remove the cake. Cool completely on a rack.

Meanwhile, for the icing, whiz all the ingredients in a food processor or beat using electric beaters until smooth. Spread over the cooled cake, then sprinkle with the remaining chopped walnuts before slicing.

Yoghurt cake with rose-scented berries

Serves 6-8

1 1/3 cups (200g) self-raising flour
1 cup (125g) almond meal
150g caster sugar
1 tsp baking powder
2 eggs, lightly beaten
250g thick Greek-style yoghurt
150ml sunflower oil
Finely grated zest of 1 small lemon
Icing sugar, to dust

Rose-scented berries
175g caster sugar
Juice of 1 lemon
1 tbs rosewater*
500g fresh or frozen mixed berries

Preheat the oven to 180°C. Grease a 20cm springform cake pan and line the base with baking paper.

Sift the flour into a bowl and add the almond meal, sugar and baking powder. Gently whisk the egg, yoghurt, oil and zest in a separate bowl, then add to the dry ingredients and stir using a wooden spoon until well combined. Pour into the cake pan and smooth the top. Bake for 30 minutes or until a skewer inserted into the centre comes out clean. Cool slightly, then remove from the pan and place on a rack to cool completely.

Meanwhile, for the rose-scented berries, place the sugar, lemon juice and 1 cup (250ml) water in a saucepan and bring to the boil, stirring to dissolve the sugar. Decrease the heat to low and simmer, without stirring, for 5 minutes until syrupy. Leave to cool, then stir in the rosewater and berries.

Just before serving, spoon some of the berries and syrup over the cake and dust with icing sugar. Serve with the remaining berries
* Rosewater is available from Middle Eastern shops and selected supermarkets.

Dulce de leche cupcakes

Makes 12

Dulce de leche is a wicked thick caramel popular in South America. You can make it yourself using condensed milk, or buy it from some delis.

125g unsalted butter, softened
1/2 tsp vanilla extract
3/4 cup (165g) caster sugar
3 eggs
2 cups (300g) self-raising flour
1/4 cup (60ml) milk
450g dulce de leche* (see Basics, p 246)

Preheat the oven to 180°C. Grease a 12-hole muffin pan or line with paper cases.

Using electric beaters, mix the butter, vanilla, sugar, eggs, flour and milk together on medium speed for 3 minutes until smooth and pale. Divide the batter among the muffin holes and bake for 25 minutes or until a skewer inserted into the centre comes out clean.

Cool cupcakes slightly in the pan, then turn out and place on a rack to cool completely. Spread the cooled cakes with dulce de leche.

* Ready-made dulce de leche is available from gourmet food shops and delis (see Glossary).

Sticky date loaf

Serves 6-8

The great thing about this loaf is that you can warm slices in the microwave and serve with toffee sauce or extra golden syrup for a cheat's version of everyone's favourite pudding!

250g pitted dates
60g unsalted butter,
   roughly chopped
180g caster sugar
2 tbs golden syrup,
   plus extra to serve
1 tsp bicarbonate of soda
2 eggs, beaten
180g plain flour, sifted
1 tsp baking powder
Cream cheese or butter,
   to spread

Preheat the oven to 170°C. Grease a 25cm x 10cm loaf pan and line with baking paper.

Place the dates and 1 cup (250ml) water in a saucepan and bring to the boil, then decrease the heat to low and simmer for 3-4 minutes until all the liquid has absorbed and the dates are mushy. Mash to break up any big pieces, then add the butter, sugar and golden syrup. Stir until the butter has melted, then remove from the heat and stir the bicarbonate of soda into the hot mixture. Cool slightly, then stir in the egg. Fold in the flour and baking powder, then spread the batter into the pan and bake for 30 minutes or until a skewer inserted into the centre comes out clean (cover loosely with foil if browning too quickly).

Cool slightly in the pan, then turn out onto a rack to cool completely. Slice and serve with cream cheese or butter to spread, and golden syrup to drizzle.

Swedish apple cake

Serves 6

2 eggs
250g caster sugar
100g unsalted butter, chopped
150ml milk
1 tsp vanilla extract
175g self-raising flour, sifted
4 small Granny Smith apples,
    peeled, cored, sliced 1cm thick
Pure (thin) cream or ice cream, to serve

Preheat the oven to 180°C. Grease a 24cm springform pan or loose-bottomed tart pan.

Place the eggs in a bowl with 200g of the sugar and use a hand whisk to combine well.

Place the butter, milk and vanilla in a saucepan over medium-low heat and cook, stirring, until the butter has melted. Slowly whisk the milk mixture into the egg mixture, then fold in the flour until combined.

Lay half the apple slices in the base of the pan. Carefully pour in the batter, then arrange the remaining apple slices on top. Sprinkle with the remaining 50g sugar, then bake for 25 minutes or until puffed and golden. Allow to cool slightly in the pan, then transfer to a platter. Serve warm with cream or ice cream.

Plum fool

Serves 6

1kg plums, halved, stones removed
Juice of 1 lemon
$^1/_2$ cup (110g) caster sugar
1 vanilla bean, split, seeds scraped
300ml thickened cream
150g ready-made custard
Ready-made meringues, to serve
Mint leaves, to garnish

Place the plums, lemon juice, sugar, vanilla pod and seeds and $^1/_4$ cup (60ml) water in a saucepan over medium heat. Poach for 10-12 minutes until the plums have softened. Remove with a slotted spoon and set aside.

Return the pan of poaching liquid to medium heat and cook, stirring, for 3-4 minutes until the syrup is reduced by half. Remove from the heat and set aside to cool.

Place the plums in a food processor (reserving a few halves to serve) and process until smooth. Transfer to a large bowl.

Lightly whip the cream, then fold into the plum puree with the custard. Chill the plum fool in the fridge for 30 minutes.

Just before serving, drizzle the plum syrup over the fool. Serve with the reserved plums, meringues and mint leaves.

Hot toddy pudding

Serves 6

Inspired by that classic winter nightcap, the hot toddy, I decided to add a couple of tablespoons of whisky to give these puddings a bit of a kick, but feel free to leave it out if you prefer. For added indulgence, serve with thick cream.

90g unsalted butter,
   at room temperature
2^1/$_3$ cups (300g) caster sugar
1^1/$_2$ cups (375ml) milk
3 eggs
^{1}/$_2$ cup (125ml) fresh lemon juice,
   plus 2 tsp finely grated lemon zest
^{1}/$_2$ cup (75g) plain flour
1 tsp baking powder
2 tbs whisky (optional)
Icing sugar, to dust
Blueberry sauce (see Basics, p 246)
   or seasonal fruit (such as rhubarb
   or mixed berries), to serve

Preheat the oven to 170°C. Lightly grease six 200ml ramekins or baking dishes.

Place the butter, sugar, milk, egg, lemon juice and zest, flour, baking powder and whisky in a food processor and process until smooth. Divide the mixture among the ramekins.

Bake for 25 minutes or until light golden. Remove from the oven and leave to stand for 5 minutes. Dust with icing sugar and serve with blueberry sauce or seasonal fruit.

Peach & ginger crumble

Serves 6

There are times when canned fruit works perfectly well in baking,
and this quick dessert is certainly one of them.

2 x 400g cans sliced peaches
    in natural juice
2 tbs chopped stem ginger in syrup*
300g good-quality ginger biscuits*
60g unsalted butter, softened
Creme anglaise (see Basics, p 246)
    or pure (thin) cream, to serve

Preheat the oven to 170°C.

Drain the peach slices, reserving $1/2$ cup (125ml) of the juice. Combine the peach, reserved juice and stem ginger in a bowl, then transfer to a shallow 1.5-litre baking dish.

Place the biscuits in a food processor and process to fine crumbs. Add the butter and pulse until the mixture resembles coarse breadcrumbs. Cover the peaches with the crumble mixture, then bake for 20 minutes or until golden and bubbling.

Serve the crumble with creme anglaise or pure cream.

* Stem ginger in syrup is available from selected supermarkets and delis. We used ginger shortbread (see Glossary).

Baked apples

Serves 4

I originally made this dessert with leftover fruit mince at Christmas, but it's so delicious it stayed on the menu at home all year. You can use mixed dried fruit if you can't find fruit mince.

4 large Granny Smith apples
80g unsalted butter, diced
1/3 firmly packed cup (65g) brown sugar
1 tsp ground cinnamon
1/2 cup fruit mince or mixed dried fruit
Pure (thin) cream, to serve

Preheat the oven to 180°C.

Core the apples, then use a sharp knife to cut a thin line around the circumference of each apple to prevent them from bursting.

Use a fork to mash the butter and sugar together in a bowl until combined. Add the cinnamon and fruit mince and stir to combine. Pack the mixture into the cavity of each apple, pressing down well.

Place apples in a baking dish (preferably one that is a snug fit) and pour 1/4 cup (60ml) water into the base of the dish. Bake for 30 minutes or until bubbling and just starting to soften.

Place the apples on 4 serving plates, drizzle over the juices from the baking dish and top with lashings of cream.

Dried apricots in amaretto with amaretti cream

Serves 6

Poached in this lovely aromatic liqueur, dried apricots take on a whole
new dimension and are a great option when fresh aren't in season.

3$^{1}/_{3}$ cups (500g) dried apricots
$^{1}/_{2}$ cup (110g) caster sugar
$^{1}/_{3}$ cup (80ml) amaretto liqueur*
100ml thickened cream
$^{1}/_{3}$ cup (95g) thick Greek-style yoghurt
50g amaretti biscuits*, crushed,
    plus extra to serve

Soak the apricots in 2 cups (500ml) boiling
water for 30 minutes.

Drain into a saucepan, setting the apricots
aside. Add the sugar to the soaking liquid, then
place over low heat and stir for 2-3 minutes
until the sugar dissolves. Increase the heat
to medium and simmer for 5-6 minutes, then
stir in the apricots and liqueur and simmer
for a further 3 minutes until syrupy. Transfer
to a bowl and cool slightly. Cover with plastic
wrap and chill until required.

Use electric beaters to whip the cream
until soft peaks form. Fold in the yoghurt and
crushed biscuits, then chill until ready to serve.

Serve the apricots topped with the cream
and sprinkled with extra crushed amaretti.
* Amaretto liqueur, made from bitter almonds
or apricot kernels, is available from bottle
shops. Amaretti biscuits are from delis and
selected supermarkets.

Almond croissant pudding with creme anglaise and raspberries

Serves 6-8

This pudding is great served warm for dessert, and is equally good the next day for breakfast.

4 almond croissants (preferably day-old), torn into large chunks
4 eggs
1/2 cup (110g) caster sugar
300ml milk
300ml pure (thin) cream
1 vanilla bean, split, seeds scraped
Finely grated zest of 1/2 orange
2 tbs brandy
Toasted flaked almonds, fresh raspberries and creme anglaise* (see Basics, p 246) or cream, to serve
Icing sugar, to dust

Grease the base and sides of a 1-litre terrine or loaf pan and line with baking paper. Pack croissants into the terrine or pan. Set aside.

Whisk the eggs and sugar together in a large bowl until just combined.

Place the milk, cream and vanilla pod and seeds in a saucepan over low heat and bring to just below boiling point, then gradually pour the warm milk mixture into the egg mixture, whisking constantly. Add the orange zest and brandy and whisk well to combine. Pour over the croissants in the terrine or loaf pan and set aside at room temperature for 1 hour so the custard soaks in – this will make for a much lighter pudding.

Preheat the oven to 180°C. Bake the pudding for 45 minutes until just set and golden on top (cover with foil if it's browning too quickly).

Allow to cool slightly, then turn out and slice. Scatter with almonds and raspberries, drizzle with creme anglaise or cream and serve dusted with icing sugar.

* Creme anglaise is also available from gourmet food shops.

Quick strawberry tarts

Makes 6

375g block frozen puff pastry, thawed
1 egg, beaten
3 tsp caster sugar
1/2 cup (160g) strawberry jam
1 cup (250g) mascarpone cheese
1 vanilla bean, split, seeds scraped
1/4 cup (40g) icing sugar, sifted,
   plus extra to dust
250g punnet strawberries, sliced
Orange zest strips and baby basil leaves
   (optional), to garnish
Flowers (optional), to decorate

Preheat the oven to 200°C.

Roll the pastry out on a lightly floured workbench to 3-5mm thick, then cut six 12cm x 5cm rectangles. Place on a lined baking tray and brush with the egg. Sprinkle with the caster sugar and top with another sheet of baking paper. Place another baking tray on top to keep the pastry flat. Bake for 15 minutes until crisp and golden. Set aside to cool.

To make a strawberry sauce, warm the jam in a saucepan over low heat, then press through a sieve, discarding any solids. Set aside.

Place the mascarpone, vanilla seeds and icing sugar in a bowl and beat until smooth.

When ready to serve, place the pastry rectangles on 6 serving plates and spread with mascarpone mixture. Top with strawberry slices and drizzle over the sauce, then sprinkle with orange zest, and baby basil and flowers if desired. Serve dusted with icing sugar.

Lavender panna cotta with lavender shards

Serves 4-6

400ml pure (thin) cream
200ml thickened cream
1/4 cup (55g) caster sugar
Pared rind of 1 lemon
1 vanilla bean, split, seeds scraped
2 tbs dried edible lavender flowers*,
    plus extra to garnish
3 gold-strength gelatine leaves*
Chocolate sauce (see Basics, p 246),
    to serve

Lavender shards
1 cup (220g) caster sugar
1 tsp dried edible lavender flowers*

Place the cream, sugar, lemon rind, vanilla pod and seeds and lavender in a saucepan over medium-low heat, stirring to dissolve the sugar. Bring to just below boiling point, then remove from heat and set aside for 30 minutes to infuse.

Soak the gelatine leaves in cold water for 5 minutes to soften. Meanwhile, reheat the cream mixture over low heat. Squeeze excess liquid from gelatine, then add leaves to cream, stirring to dissolve. Strain mixture through a sieve, pressing down on lavender flowers to extract as much flavour as possible. Divide among four to six 150ml serving glasses, then chill for at least 4 hours, preferably overnight.

Meanwhile, for lavender shards, lightly grease a baking sheet. Stir sugar and 1/2 cup (125ml) water in a saucepan over low heat to dissolve. Increase heat to high and bring to the boil, then allow to bubble, not stirring but occasionally brushing sides down with a wet pastry brush, for 5-6 minutes until golden. Pour onto tray, scatter with lavender and set aside at room temperature for 10 minutes or until set. Crack into shards, then store in an airtight container for 2-3 days.

Top each panna cotta with a little chocolate sauce, then add lavender shards and garnish with extra lavender flowers.
* Lavender flowers (see Glossary) and gelatine leaves are available from gourmet food shops and selected delis. Check gelatine packet for setting instructions.

White chocolate mojito cheesecakes

Serves 6

I have to thank Angela Boggiano, my counterpart at UK *delicious.*, for the inspiration behind these simple trifles. My addition of some melted white chocolate just gilds the lily.

20g unsalted butter, melted
150g good-quality ginger biscuits*,
   crushed in a food processor
$1/2$ cup (110g) caster sugar
Finely grated zest and juice of 3 limes,
   plus 1 thinly sliced lime to garnish
100ml white rum
1 cup mint leaves, plus extra to garnish
120g white chocolate, chopped
400g soft cream cheese
1 cup (250g) mascarpone cheese
300ml thickened cream, whipped
Slivered unsalted pistachios, to garnish
Borage flowers (optional), to decorate

Stir the melted butter into the biscuit crumbs until well combined. Press the mixture into the base of 6 serving glasses (use a cocktail muddling stick or the end of a rolling pin to pack down well). Chill in the fridge.

Place the sugar and $1/4$ cup (60ml) water in a saucepan. Bring to the boil, stirring to dissolve the sugar, then reduce heat to medium-low and simmer for 5 minutes until syrupy. Add the lime zest and juice, rum and mint. Remove from heat. Set aside for 20 minutes to infuse.

Meanwhile, place the chocolate in a heatproof bowl over a pan of simmering water (don't let the bowl touch the water). Stir gently until melted, then set aside to cool.

Clean the food processor, then add the cream cheese and mascarpone and process to combine. Strain the syrup through a sieve, pressing down to extract as much flavour as possible, then add the syrup to the processor and process to combine. Add the chocolate and pulse 2-3 times until incorporated. Spoon the mixture into the glasses. Chill for 1 hour to set.

When ready to serve, top each glass with some whipped cream. Garnish with lime slices, slivered pistachios and extra mint, then decorate with flowers if desired.

* We used ginger shortbread (see Glossary).

Grand Marnier crepe layer cake

Serves 8-10

Despite its spectacular appearance, this is actually easy to make (especially if you use bought frozen crepes, or make them ahead and freeze them) and will certainly impress guests.

125g unsalted butter, melted, cooled

1 quantity crepe batter
    (see Basics, p 246)

600ml thickened cream

3/4 cup (120g) pure icing sugar,
    plus extra to dust

2 tsp grated orange zest

1/4 cup (60ml) Grand Marnier

1 tsp vanilla extract

1 quantity orange sauce
    (see Basics, p 246)

Grease a 20cm springform cake pan and line the base with baking paper.

For the crepes, heat a 20cm crepe pan or small frypan over medium heat and brush with a little melted butter. Add 1/4 cup (60ml) of the crepe batter and swirl to coat the base. Cook for 2 minutes each side until just golden. Repeat with remaining batter to make about 30 crepes, stacking with baking paper between the layers. Set aside.

To make the filling, place the cream, icing sugar, orange zest, Grand Marnier and vanilla extract in a bowl. Beat with electric beaters until stiff peaks form.

To assemble the cake, layer the crepes, spreading each with a thin layer of cream mixture and finishing with a crepe. Cover and chill for at least 4 hours until set.

Transfer the cake to a serving platter, then cut into slices and serve drizzled with orange sauce and dusted with extra icing sugar.

Coconut ice cream with lime & mint syrup

Serves 6

2 cups (140g) shredded coconut
1L coconut ice cream*
Tropical and seasonal fruits (such
   as kiwifruit, star fruit, papaya
   and mango), sliced, to serve

Lime & mint syrup
1 cup (220g) caster sugar
Grated zest of 2 limes
1/3 cup mint leaves,
   plus sprigs to garnish

Toast the shredded coconut in a dry frypan over medium-low heat, stirring, for 1-2 minutes until golden. Remove from the pan and cool.

Scoop the ice cream into balls, roll in the toasted coconut to coat and freeze on a lined baking tray for about 1 hour until firm.

Meanwhile, to make the lime and mint syrup, place the sugar, lime zest, mint leaves and 1 cup (250ml) water in a saucepan over medium heat. Stir until the sugar dissolves, then bring to a simmer and cook for 3 minutes or until slightly thickened and syrupy. Remove from the heat and set aside to cool, then strain and discard the lime zest and mint leaves.

Serve the ice cream balls on a platter with the fruit, mint leaves and a little syrup poured over.
* Available from delis and ice cream shops. Substitute good-quality vanilla ice cream.

Orange marmalade ice cream

Serves 6-8

It's amazing how delicious and creamy this ice cream is – even without eggs. An ice cream machine is a great quick option for churning, but the hand-beaten method works just as well.

250g good-quality Seville orange
  marmalade
300ml thickened cream
300ml thick Greek-style yoghurt
1/4 cup (60ml) fresh orange juice

Place the marmalade, cream, yoghurt and orange juice in a bowl and whisk to combine.

Churn in an ice cream machine following manufacturer's directions. Alternatively, pour the mixture into a shallow container and freeze for 2-3 hours until frozen at the edges. Remove from the freezer and beat with electric beaters, then refreeze. Repeat this process two or three times.

Serve with fresh fruit or biscotti.

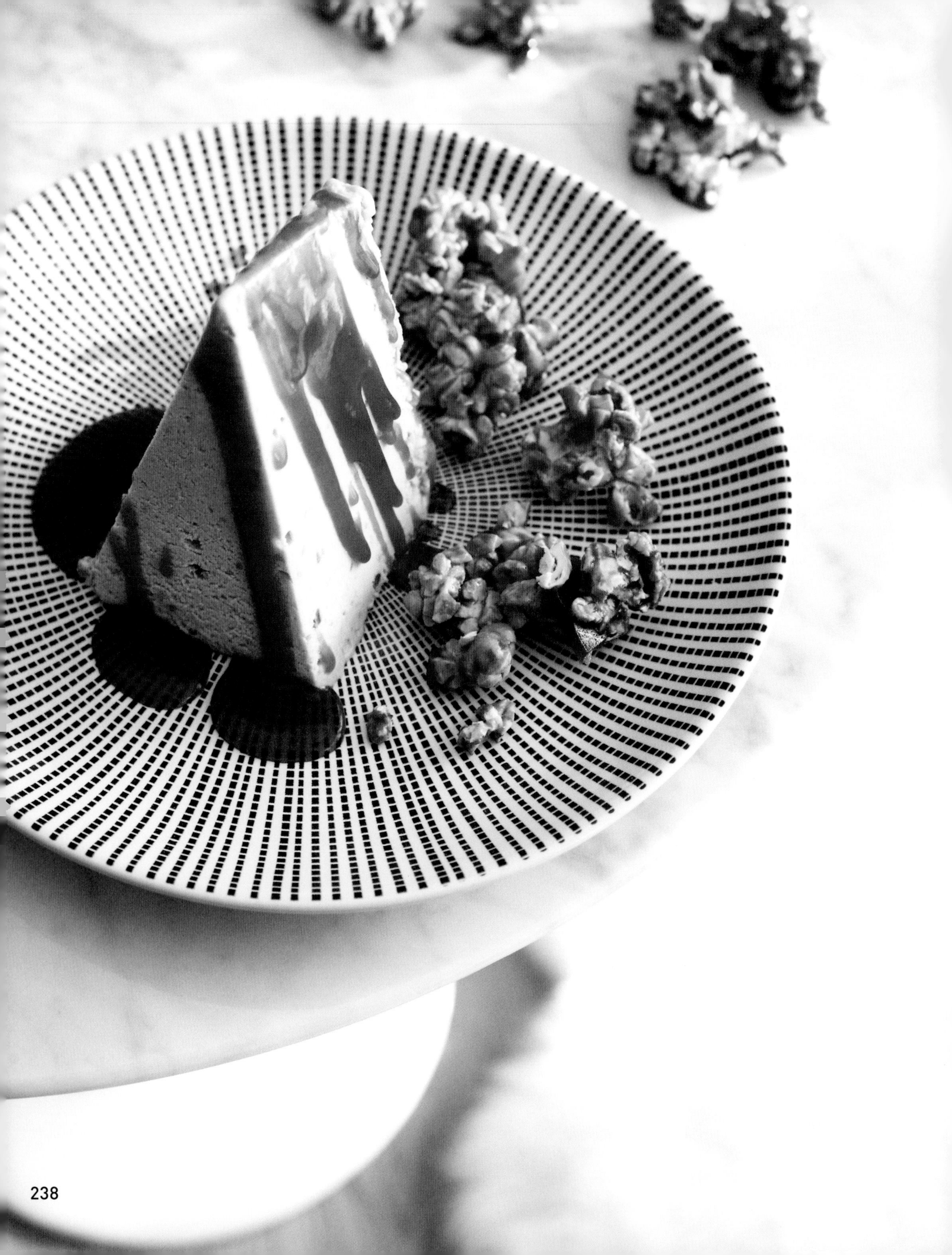

Peanut butter ice cream with caramel popcorn brittle

Serves 6-8

1L good-quality vanilla ice cream,
   softened
1 cup (280g) crunchy peanut butter
1 cup (220g) caster sugar
20g unsalted butter
100g pack microwave popcorn,
   cooked to instructions
2/3 cup (100g) salted peanuts, crushed
Caramel sauce (see Basics, p 246),
   to serve

Place the ice cream and peanut butter in a food processor and pulse to combine. Pour into a lined 1-litre terrine mould or loaf pan and freeze for at least 4 hours or until firm.

Place sugar and 100ml water in a saucepan over low heat, bring to a simmer and stir to dissolve the sugar. Cook for 6-8 minutes, watching carefully, until it becomes a light caramel colour. Add the butter, popcorn and peanuts, stirring quickly to coat (the mixture will seize, but continue cooking over medium-low heat until the caramel is smooth again), then stir in 1/2 teaspoon sea salt.

Spread the mixture onto a sheet of baking paper. When cool enough to handle, break the caramel popcorn into small shards.

Turn out the terrine and slice the ice cream into wedges. Serve with the popcorn shards, drizzled with caramel sauce.

Lemon & raspberry ripple gelato

Serves 4-6

250g raspberries

$^1/_3$ cup (50g) pure icing sugar, sifted

$^3/_4$ cup (185ml) fresh lemon juice,
   plus 1 tsp grated lemon zest

185g caster sugar

$^1/_4$ cup (60ml) light corn syrup

$^1/_2$ tsp vanilla extract

1kg vanilla-flavoured yoghurt or
   sweetened thick Greek-style yoghurt

Whiz the raspberries and icing sugar together in a food processor to form a puree. Pass through a fine sieve, then set sauce aside.

Combine lemon juice and zest, caster sugar, corn syrup and vanilla extract in a bowl. Add the yoghurt and mix well to combine.

Churn in an ice cream machine following manufacturer's directions until just frozen, then transfer to a 1.5-litre container and use a skewer to make lines down the ice cream. Pour over half the raspberry sauce (reserving the rest to serve), then use the skewer to swirl in a decorative pattern. Freeze until firm.

Alternatively, pour mixture into a shallow container and freeze for 2-3 hours until frozen at the edges. Remove from freezer and beat with electric beaters, then refreeze. Repeat this process two or three times until thick and frozen, swirling through the rasperry sauce after the final beating.

Serve scoops of the gelato drizzled with the remaining raspberry puree.

Choc-ice meringues with hot white chocolate sauce

Serves 4

200g good-quality dark chocolate,
    chopped
50ml freshly brewed espresso coffee
400g ready-made custard
300ml thickened cream
4 ready-made meringue nests
Cocoa powder, to dust

White chocolate sauce
75g white chocolate, chopped
100ml pure (thin) cream

Place chocolate and coffee in a heatproof bowl over a saucepan of simmering water (don't let the bowl touch the water) and stir until melted and smooth. Remove from heat. In a separate bowl combine the custard and thickened cream, then stir in the chocolate mixture.

Churn in an ice cream machine following manufacturer's directions. Alternatively, pour the mixture into a shallow container and freeze for 2-3 hours until frozen at the edges. Remove from the freezer and beat with electric beaters, then refreeze. Repeat this process two or three times.

Just before serving, make the chocolate sauce. Place the chocolate and cream in a heatproof bowl over a saucepan of simmering water (don't let the bowl touch the water) and stir until melted and smooth. Keep warm.

Place the meringues on 4 serving plates, then top each with a scoop of the chocolate ice cream. Dust with cocoa powder and drizzle with the warm chocolate sauce.

basics

BLUEBERRY SAUCE
Makes 1 1/2 cups

150g blueberries
1/2 cup (110g) caster sugar
100ml dry Marsala*
1 cinnamon quill
1 tsp arrowroot*

Place berries, sugar, Marsala, cinnamon and 1/2 cup (125ml) water in a saucepan over low heat, stir to dissolve sugar, then simmer for 5 minutes. Mix arrowroot with 1 tbs cold water, add to pan and cook for a further 1-2 minutes until thickened. Remove from heat and set aside to cool.
* Marsala is available from bottle shops. Arrowroot (a thickening agent) is available from supermarkets.

CARAMEL SAUCE
Makes 1 cup

50g unsalted butter
1/2 firmly packed cup (100g) brown sugar
3 tbs golden syrup
150ml thickened cream
1 tsp vanilla extract

Place all the ingredients in a pan over low heat, stir to dissolve sugar, then simmer for 5 minutes until thickened. Serve warm or cold.

CHOCOLATE SAUCE
Makes 1 1/2 cups

200ml pure (thin) cream
50ml milk
200g dark chocolate, chopped
20g good-quality cocoa powder

Place cream and milk in a saucepan over medium heat. Bring to just below boiling point, then remove from heat. Whisk in chocolate until melted, then gently whisk in cocoa until smooth. Strain into a jug and set aside to cool.

CREME ANGLAISE
Makes 2 1/2 cups

4 egg yolks
1 cup (250ml) milk
1 cup (250ml) pure (thin) cream
1/4 cup (55g) caster sugar
1 tsp vanilla extract

Lightly beat egg yolks in a bowl. Place milk, cream, sugar and vanilla in a saucepan over medium heat and bring to just below boiling point. Pour hot milk mixture over egg yolks, whisking constantly, then return to the pan over very low heat. Stir constantly with a wooden spoon for 5-6 minutes until the custard is thick enough to coat the back of the spoon. Pour into a jug, cover surface closely with plastic wrap to prevent a skin forming, then chill until needed.

CREPES
Makes 30

2 cups (300g) plain flour
1 tsp baking powder
2 tbs pure icing sugar
4 eggs
450ml milk
1 cup (250ml) pure (thin) cream
1/2 tsp vanilla extract
100g unsalted butter, melted, cooled

Process all ingredients except butter in a food processor until smooth, pour into a jug and stand for 30 minutes at room temperature. Heat a 20cm crepe pan or small frypan over medium heat and brush with a little butter. Add 1/4 cup (60ml) of the crepe batter and swirl to coat the base. Cook for 2 minutes each side until just golden. Repeat with remaining batter, brushing the pan with a little butter each time, to make about 30 crepes, stacking with baking paper in between. Crepes can be frozen for up to 3 months.

DUCK-FAT FRIED POTATOES
Serves 4 as a side

4 potatoes (such as King Edward), peeled, cut into 2cm pieces
2 tbs duck fat
2 tbs chopped flat-leaf parsley

Cook potatoes in boiling salted water for 3 minutes. Drain and return to pan (the warmth will help to dry the potato). Melt the fat in a frypan over medium-high heat. When hot, cook the potato, turning to brown evenly, for 8-10 minutes until golden. Season, then stir in parsley.

DULCE DE LECHE
Makes 1 1/2 cups

2 x 395g cans sweetened condensed milk

Remove and discard labels from milk cans, then make 2 small holes in the top of each with a can opener. Place in a saucepan, opened-side up, and add enough water to almost cover cans.

Bring to the boil, then adjust heat to a gentle simmer and cook for 3 hours, topping up with boiling water so it stays at the same level. Using an oven glove, carefully remove cans from water. Cool completely, then open cans and scoop the thick caramel out into a container.

GARLIC BREAD
Serves 4-6

1 baguette
150g unsalted butter, softened
4 garlic cloves
1/2 cup flat-leaf parsley leaves

Preheat oven to 180°C. Slice baguette 2cm thick, without cutting all the way through. Whiz remaining ingredients in a processor with salt and pepper until well combined. Spread bread with garlic butter, enclose in foil and bake for 10 minutes, then open foil and bake for 2 minutes until golden.

GREEN PAPAYA SALAD
Serves 4

1 long red chilli, seeds removed, finely chopped
2 garlic cloves, chopped
2 tbs grated palm sugar*
Juice of 1 lime
1 tbs tamarind concentrate*
2 tbs fish sauce
3 cups shredded green papaya
1/4 cup chopped coriander
1/4 cup chopped mint

Place chilli, garlic and sugar in a mortar and pestle and pound to a smooth paste. Stir in juice, tamarind and sauce. Toss in

a bowl with papaya and herbs. Mix well.
* Available from Asian food shops.

ORANGE SAUCE
Makes 1 1/2 cups

250g caster sugar
Zest of 2 oranges
1/2 cup (125ml) Grand Marnier

Place sugar and 100ml water in a pan over low heat and stir to dissolve sugar. Increase heat to medium and simmer, not stirring, for 6-8 minutes until a golden toffee colour (watch carefully, as it burns easily). Remove from heat and carefully (it may spit) add 150ml boiling water and zest. Return to medium-low heat and cook, stirring, for 2-3 minutes until combined and thickened. Add Grand Marnier and swirl to combine. Cool.

PAN-FRIED POTATOES WITH CHORIZO
Serves 4-6

800g small potatoes (such as chats or kipflers), peeled, thickly sliced
100ml olive oil
1 onion, thinly sliced
200g chorizo, chopped
4 garlic cloves, thinly sliced
1 tsp smoked paprika (pimenton)*
2 bay leaves
1/2 cup (125ml) dry white wine
Chopped flat-leaf parsley, to serve

Cook potato in boiling salted water for 3 minutes. Drain and return to the pan (the warmth will help to dry the potato). Heat oil in a frypan over medium heat. Cook onion and chorizo, stirring, for

3-5 minutes until onion softens. Add potato, garlic, paprika, bay, wine and 100ml water and cook for 8-10 minutes until all liquid is absorbed and potato is tender, then cook for a further 2 minutes until crisp. Sprinkle with parsley.
* From gourmet shops and delis.

PICO DE GALLO
Makes 2 cups

2 vine-ripened tomatoes, seeds removed, thinly sliced
1 small red onion, thinly sliced
4 long green chillies, seeds removed, thinly sliced
1 cup chopped coriander leaves
2 garlic cloves, finely chopped
Juice of 2 limes
1/4 cup (60ml) olive oil
1 tsp ground cumin

Mix all ingredients in a bowl with salt and pepper. Serve with grilled fish or meats.

SOFT POLENTA
Serves 4-6

300ml milk
1 garlic clove, crushed
100g instant polenta
1/2 cup (125ml) pure (thin) cream
30g grated parmesan
100g mascarpone cheese

Place milk, garlic, 200ml water and 1 tsp salt in a pan, season and bring to the boil. Whisk in polenta and cook, stirring, for 2 minutes until thickened. Stir in cream and parmesan and warm through over low heat. Remove from heat and stir through mascarpone. Season to taste.

menus

SUNDAY BEST

52

Pea & pea shoot soup with coriander & sweet chilli cream

+

158

Shortcut roast lamb with caramelised onion couscous

+

220

Baked apples

ALFRESCO

31

Heirloom tomato stacks with basil oil

+

93

Whole baked salmon with wasabi tartare

+

227

Quick strawberry tarts

MIDWEEK SPECIAL

114

Kumara galettes

+

178

Swedish meatballs

+

195

Classic chocolate pots

glossary

Panch phora (p 24)
Herbie's Spices, (02) 9555 6035, herbies.com.au.
Lingonberry sauce (p 178)
Ikea: Vic (03) 8416 5000, NSW (02) 8002 0400,
Qld (07) 3380 6800, ikea.com.au.
Moroccan spice mix (p 129)
Herbie's Spices, (02) 9555 6035, herbies.com.au
Chermoula paste (p 86)
Greg Malouf, gregmalouf.com.au;
or Christine Manfield, christinemanfield.com.
Good-quality ginger biscuits (p 219, 231)
Duchy Original Ginger Shortbread from Simon Johnson,
1800 655 522, simonjohnson.com.au.
Dried edible lavender flowers (p 228)
Herbie's Spices, (02) 9555 6035, herbies.com.au;
or The Essential Ingredient, essentialingredient.com.au.
Ras el hanout (p 133)
Greg Malouf, gregmalouf.com.au.
Harissa paste (p 105)
Christine Manfield, christinemanfield.com;
Simon Johnson, 1800 655 522, simonjohnson.com.au; or
Thomas Dux Grocer, (02) 8885 6666, thomasdux.com.au.
Chocolate shortcrust pastry (p 196)
Carême Dark Chocolate Shortcrust Pastry.
For stockists, visit: caremepastry.com.
Dulce de leche (p 209)
Latin Passions Confectionery Premium Caramel Spread,
(03) 9357 4481, latinpassions.com.au.

THANKS TO THE FOLLOWING STOCKISTS:
Bison Australia (02) 6257 7255, bisonhome.com
Mud Australia (02) 9389 5580, mudaustralia.com
Design Mode International 1800 084 258
iittala iittala.com
Smeg Appliances (02) 9384 5678, smegappliances.com.au
Top 3 by Design 1300 867 333, top3.com.au

thanks

I am always amazed at the sheer slog that goes into putting a cookbook together – from those first initial ideas about recipes, to the effort and involvement of a small group of people who have all worked tirelessly to put *Quick Smart Cook* together (and, for many of us, to get a magazine and a few other publications out at the same time!)

So, where to start with my thanks... obviously to Sandra Hook, Fiona Nilsson and the rest of the management team at News Magazines for giving me the opportunity to create this latest *delicious.* cookbook. To editor-in-chief Trudi Jenkins for your continued support, advice and encouragement. And to Shona Martyn, Brigitta Doyle, Michelle Weisz and the team at ABC Books/HarperCollins, once again for your support, enthusiasm and sound advice along the way.

And where would I be without the fantastic editorial team at delicious., including editor Kylie Walker, senior subeditor Sarah Macdonald, Alison Pickel, Amanda Vallis and superwoman Danielle Oppermann – our wonderful deputy editor whose eagle eyes scour my every word and who successfully manages to hold everything together under stress and still come up smiling. Thanks, too, to Molly Furzer for joining us for another 'cookbook season'.

Many thanks to the art team, with our extremely talented creative director Scott Cassidy at the helm, and designers Simon Martin and Elizabeth Lough (yes, I know I made lots of changes) – you've all done such a great job in making every page look so delicious!

Shooting a book is never easy, but the job was made so much more fun working with such a talented photographer and stylist. Brett Stevens' incredible images (how do you get those shafts of light in the shots?) and David Morgan's vision and dedication were invaluable. Thanks for putting up with my many changes of heart... I hope you'll agree it was worth it in the end.

And I must thank our senior food assistant Georgina Kaveney, who was in the kitchen with me day after day working tirelessly to make the food look good, as well as Phoebe Wood (the new kid on the block), who was thrown in at the deep end.

Last but not least, thanks to my family – Phil, Toby and Henry – who put up with me regardless. Life can get back to normal now for a while...

The *delicious.* trademark is used under licence from The Australian Broadcasting Corporation and News Magazines.

Published by HarperCollins Publishers Ltd
Originally published in Australia in 2009 by HarperCollins*Publishers* Pty Limited.

First Canadian edition

HarperCollins books may be purchased for educational, business, or sales promotional use through our Special Markets Department.

HarperCollins Publishers Ltd
2 Bloor Street East, 20th Floor
Toronto, Ontario, Canada
M4W 1A8

www.harpercollins.ca

Library and Archives Canada Cataloguing in Publication information is available upon request

ISBN: 978-1-44343-171-2

Food Director Valli Little **Photography** Brett Stevens (Ben Dearnley p 6, Mark Roper p 151) **Styling** David Morgan **Creative Director** Scott Cassidy **Designers** Elizabeth Lough, Simon Martin **Project Editors** Molly Furzer, Sarah Macdonald, Danielle Oppermann **Food Preparation** Georgina Kaveney, Phoebe Wood *delicious.* **Editor-in-chief** Trudi Jenkins *delicious.* **Editor** Kylie Walker **CEO, News Magazines** Sandra Hook

Printed and bound in Canada
9 8 7 6 5 4 3 2 1